GRIT
for the Pearl

Mandolen Mull

Copyright © 2024 by Mandolen Mull

Grit for the Pearl
Published by MullMentum Consulting
P.O. Box 123
Oregon, Illinois 61061
www.mullmentum.com

All rights reserved. No part of this publication may be reproduced, distributed, or transmitted in any form or by any means, including photocopying, recording, or other electronic or mechanical methods, without the prior written permission of the publisher, except in the case of brief quotations embodied in critical reviews and certain other noncommercial uses permitted by copyright law. For permission requests, write to the publisher, addressed 'Attention: Permissions Coordinator,' at the address above.

ISBN 979-8-9912687-0-7 (Paperback)
ISBN 979-8-9912687-1-4 (Hard Case)
eISBN 979-8-9912687-2-1 (ePub)

Cover design by Shonda Ramsey

Printed in the United States of America
First Edition 2024

10 9 8 7 6 5 4 3 2 1

082024

Table of Contents

Preface 05
Author LinkedIn Bio 11
Acknowledgements 15
Intro 17
Fall 2023 19
Winter 2023 55
Spring 2024 85
Summer 2024 139
References 193
Stay Tuned 195

Preface

In 1990 famed drummer John Densmore wrote a book titled *"Riders on the Storm: My Life with Jim Morrison and The Doors"*.

About a decade later I read that book and there, in the two paragraphed preface, he left an indelible mark on me. *"This book is my truth. It may not be the whole truth, but it is the way I saw it. From the drum stool."*

What follows in the pages of this book is my truth. It may not be the whole truth, but it is the way I saw it. The way I felt it. The way I lived it. The way I've tried to make sense of it.
Indeed, the way I saw it.
From the eyes of a stone mason's daughter.
Trying to shape the jagged, rough, sharp edges of stumbling blocks into a pathway of stepping stones.

As such, I've not, as many autobiographers do, provided an advanced copy of this memoir to the individuals who are described and discussed within. Part of my healing journey is to break free of being a People Pleaser, a Perfectionist, a Person Who Asks Permission.
Through that, I have realised that I do not need permission to tell my story as I've lived it.

Another part of my healing journey has been to see people in their totality. To love their complexities.
I believe I've compassionately captured that robustness amidst the messiness. But that will be for others, from their "drum stools", to determine. It will be their truth, not mine.
And as I've learned throughout the experiences I memorialise here, myriad truths can coexist.

The messiness I've captured is also portrayed to you, dear reader, as I've opted not to organise the vignettes contained in this book other than to present them in the sequence of which I first shared them on a public forum: LinkedIn. The experiences take place over my lifetime, yet I wrote them over a period of a year.
I didn't realise I was writing a book...
The catalyst of my sharing was concurrent with healing work that continues to this day. That catalyst? Sitting in a room being told to conform.
To be a People Pleaser.
To be a Perfectionist.
To be a Person Who Seeks Permission.
"No one needs or wants to hear your story, Mandolen."

That felt fundamentally wrong to me. So, I took my story to a public platform because, frankly, I had a lot of healing to do and therapy was taking too long.
I posted daily.
I stayed true to my personal values of *Authenticity, Transparency, Courage, Accountability, Grace,* and *Growth*.
And, eventually, my vulnerability grew.

I had no intention of finding friends, a following, a family through the story I shared.
But I did.
And through the unbelievably supportive community I have found on a platform designed for business and a medium designated for superficiality, I have been encouraged to take the snippets of my story and craft them into a book.
As I look back over this past year, I am surprised and humbled to discover I have several to share.
This is the first book of the collection.
Many of my LinkedIn friends commented that they felt they were arriving in the middle of a story, and thus then went in search of story origins.
Only, they were surprised to find there was no "beginning".
There is still no "end".

There is just a group of us sharing our coffee each morning as we try to navigate this world together.
A social media tool used for the very best purpose: To help folks truly see each other.

I wrote about navigating my health issues (which this book covers). About the grief of losing my father (My Heart Sits With Yours). About the family my work created (Batten Down the Lashes). About the healing power of my Haven in the Woods and becoming an unexpected foster mother overnight (Haven & Harbour). And all along the way I shared my leadership insights (the title of which I'm still working on).
Each week my posts would be an assortment of topics because I had no actual strategy. I just sat down with a cup of coffee and wrote.
I wrote what I was feeling.
What I was observing.
What I was still trying to learn.
This book is messy.
Because my posts were messy.
Because life is messy.
This book is unedited.
Because my posts were unedited.
Because life is unedited.
This book contradicts itself.
Because as I wrote, I felt contradictory things.
Because life is a contradiction.

In the pages that follow you'll find snapshots of my life.
The times where I wrote with great optimisim.
The times where I was overwhelmed with pain.
Balancing the tension of life, I swayed from side to side, sometimes spilling out.
This memoir honours the adversities and achievements of my life thus far and introduces you to the stories that are forthcoming in my next four books in the collection.

The title, *Grit for the Pearl*, is meaningful in multiple ways.

First, my beloved Nana always told me, *"There's nothing that good heels, perfume, and pearls cannot fix."*

I have found that advice to be immensely helpful in giving me the confidence and courage I've needed to reframe my challenges into celebrations.

Another reason?

You'll have to keep reading this preface to find out.

The third?

Page 22 reveals that.

I have nominally edited the vignettes from their original posts, although I did remove the accompanying photos I used as anchoring for the reader to hear my voice throughout my writings.

The vignettes are presented in the sequence as I wrote them by season. Thus, some stories contain repetitive information, but in their redundancy a new lens or layer of my perspective- from the eyes of a stone mason's daughter- is uncovered.

As well, I added a few more stories that I'd not yet been ready to share.

Oh, also, I collected these stories and prepared this book for publishing in a week.

True to my nature, I needed a push to get past my old People-Pleasing, Perfectionist, Permission-Seeking ways.

Enter Scott MacGregor, the inimitable and fascinating founder of *The Outlier Project*, of which I'm a grateful member.

Scott challenged our group to the first ever **World Outlier Week** for the last week of June 2024.

Our task was to do something utterly Outlierish.

To break out of our comfort zones.

To be brave and bold.

To dare.

And for weeks I flustered and floundered over what I could possibly do.

Then it hit me- it was time for me to just go ahead and write the book I'd been telling everyone I was writing!

To get past my fears of what people close to me may think if they read it.

To get past the condemnation of my poor sentence structure, grammar, and colloquial sayings.

To get past my own inner critic that what I'm sharing is too personal, too vulnerable, too raw and thus too irresponsibly receptive to rejection.

To get past the shame that someone will weaponise my story- from the eyes of the stone mason's daughter- as fodder for their mean reviews and criticisms.

To get past the pain and to open myself up to the possibility that someone will once again tell me that my story doesn't matter.

The title of this book was suggested by a fellow *Outlier*, the brilliant and joy-filled Mark Holden, in the comments of the post I present to you on page 21 of this book. He felt that my story was worthy enough to not only be a book, but to be a book he wanted to share with his amazing daughters as one of inspiration and aspiration.

And so, I write this book for them, those incredible future *Outliers* in the making.

Happy Growing,
-M.

#MullMentum
#NarrativeLeadership
#GenerationalMentorship

Author LinkedIn Bio

Author LinkedIn Bio

Dr. Mandolen Mull is the Founder and Principal Consultant at MullMentum Consulting, LLC, a bespoke leadership development firm that fosters sustainable growth for individuals, teams, and organizations. With a Ph.D. in organizational development and change, and an MBA in international business, she provides analysis and interventions that improve enduring organizational performance outcomes. Leveraging her many years of experience as a professional consultant, a higher education administrator, and an operations leader throughout various industries, Mandolen uses her robust background to connect with myriad audiences- with a bit of humor and Texas Rangers talk thrown in!

As a Leadership Consultant, she specializes in customized training and mentoring programs that leverage her authentic and resonating style. She has helped clients all over the globe, from union building trades to healthcare executives, gain tools to ensure their continued leadership legacies. She is also a keynote and motivational speaker, a multiple award winner, and an author of a no-holds-barred book on the messiness and responsibility of leadership. Believing that everyone deserves to be developed, Mandolen is devoted to empowering others to achieve their full potential and make a positive impact in the world.

Mandolen enjoys balancing the line between scholar and practitioner, and utilizes her skills as a consultant, researcher, and professor to bridge the vast gap of traditional thinking and what actually takes place in the workforce. Despite navigating severe Crohn's disease and acquired torsion dystonia, Mandolen has risen to all of her 4'11 height to not only build a successful career, but to help others along the way. An advocate for invisible illnesses, recovering Formerly Ambitious People, and just anyone dealing with burnout and ready for some #Mullivation, Mandolen is currently publishing the first in a series collection of her autobiography, *"Grit for the Pearl"*.

LinkedIn: www.linkedin.com/in/Mandolen
Contact Info: www.MullMentum.com

Acknowledgements

To my family, the medical specialists, the students, the mentees, the colleagues, and the friends along this path, I thank you. The upcoming books will show more of your stories and your immense and indelible impact on my own.

To the doctor who tracked me down when I ghosted you for three weeks; who never gave up on me and believed in me more than I believed in myself; who has cried alongside me with my joys and my sorrows; who, I suspect, saw some of your own story within mine- I will never be able to convey just how much you've changed my life for the better. I am here today because of you.

To the therapist who lets me have goofy inside jokes, please know that the good, healing, parts of this story are because of your work.

To the other therapist who pushes me just enough for growth but brings me back to comfort when things get too scratchy, thank you for seeing me and letting me heal at my pace.

To the quirky doctor who makes me laugh with your cavalier, hilarious, asides and yet also marvel at your brilliance and doggedness in helping me, thank you for giving me a fighting chance to keep living this crazy life at the quality I deserve.

To the nutritionist who has literally kept me going the past several years, thank you for believing me and believing in me.

To the Bestie Rachelle Blitch- if my heart could speak, you'd know just how very, very, grateful I am to have you pave this road alongside me. And yes, my outpouring of love and appreciation would undoubtedly "make it weird" and make you (more) awkward and uncomfortable. Deal with it.

To Brooke Tomman, Anna Jattowski, Sue Hart, Christian Pearcy, Rhonda Weitzel, Jeff Allen, Renee Just, Jeff Karlberg, The Outliers, and my IronWorkers, ya'll give me such comfort and strength.

To Shonda Ramsey with Lilian Grace Designs, thank you so very much for capturing the totality of my experiences through your phenomenal cover artwork.

To my LinkedIn friends: You've not only given me a space for my voice, but you've encouraged me to "say it louder". So many of you have consistently championed my journey and in doing so, you've become an amazing community that I look forward to chatting with each morning.

I simply, authentically, sincerely, cannot articulate just how grateful I am for each of you.

Yet I would be wholly remiss if I didn't specifically thank a cadre of that family: Dean Wiener, Neil Burch, Lisa Galanter, Sean Keller, James Gibbons, Kimberly Arnold, Rich Ermlick, Jim King, Ryan Schneidmiller, Traci Austin, Rev. Joseph Calandra, Cara Houser, Doug Skoke, Elizabeth Wesley, Jake Ray, Wanda Fox, Kirby Lee, Rebecca Spadafore, Matthew Eaton, Linzy Elizabeth, Kofi Douhadji, Amanda Stern, Allison Stogdale, Richard Mascolo, Lindsay Ruiz, Ngoc Tran, Sam Ochstien, Yarrow Spitzfaden, Danny Lingenfelter, James Arbizu, Victoria Walling, Jon Dominguez, Caroline Holmyard, Jeff Williamson, Jennifer Kellett, Allison Hope Barron, Sue Michaelson, Ron Godier, Jimmy Helmick, Peter Shannon, and last but not least, the peerlessly incomparable J. Scot Heathman. You all believed in me- believe in me- and have given me such comfort and courage.
I am indebted to your kindness.
Four more to go...

Intro

Grind. Grit. Mind over matter. That all works until your mind pushes you past the things that matter.

Past sleep.
Past nourishment.
Past meaningful relationships.

I lived that life. I was **REWARDED** for that life. I joked that: "*GRIT* stands for Girl Raised In Texas!"

'Kid, you've got folks counting on you to make sound decisions. You won't mean to, but you're bound for a big mistake. Your brain isn't getting enough of what it needs- food, sleep, some downtime- for it to work as it should. You're going to end up making decisions that get folks hurt.' That's what my father said to me before I went to the hospital malnourished and with failing kidneys, to get on a feeding tube.
I worked from my hospital bed.
And we have all these hardcore folks telling us to push past any signals our body or environment gives us. We are to "master our minds".
As if that is ever a sustainable strategy.

You know what is sustainable, though? Grace.
It's taken me a very long time to learn that Grit is merely an agent for the Pearl I'm forming.
It's not actually my desired outcome.
And Grace is the safe incubator of where it all happens.

So, to the folks screaming about #GrindMentality into our newsfeeds everyday, as if we're all bound to be some Jack Ryan/Jack Reacher sidekick,

I'll take a pass. There's enough hard, harsh, mean, rugged, jagged, jarring, bone-crushing, painful things in this world without me making myself as such.
I don't want to be a diamond.
I want to be a Pearl.

Grit, sure.
Grace, absolutely.

Fall 2023

One

A family member was recently diagnosed with Crohn's and it had me thinking about how I navigated those early days.

It wasn't pretty.

It was an adjustment to realise I'd be sick the rest of my life and for a while I thought all my dreams had been taken from me.

But they weren't-I just had to learn to reframe my illnesses to be a stepping stone rather than a stumbling block.

Nothing I've endured stopped me from pursuing a career of helping others. In many respects, I was better conditioned for the inevitable hills and valleys that we all walk through in life.

I'm often asked today how I keep a positive disposition after enduring not only Crohn's and dystonia, but a miscarriage, a traumatic car wreck, and my ever ongoing battle with hypoglycaemia of which my doctors can not yet ascertain the cause (I'm drinking cornstarch these days as I dart from client to client...it is, I'm hoping, an acquired taste at some point!).

I've had over 20 scopes, 12 melanomas and 1 basal cell carcinoma, surgeries, biopsies, scans, really crazy tests (strapped to a tilt table with electrodes zapping my skin, 72-hr water fast, ingesting radioactive eggs)- to name a few.

I've had kind medical providers who comfort, and those who don't read my chart beforehand which leads to tears.

I've had people offer sympathy and others skeptically wonder if my health is really an issue as I "look and act fine".

...And I don't really care about any of that.

Because you see, none of that detracts from me.

What it did was give me an opportunity to shine light on the dark areas of shame that many people with chronic illness feel.

It allows me the chance to share my story to help others not feel so alone.

And, it gives me the chance to tell my family member:

I **KNOW** this sucks, and the first year is the hardest, but I **PROMISE** you that you were made for something great.

This is part of your journey and it will make you and others better.

Anything that emits light must first endure burning.

And your light is about to shine.

Two

"I had a hysterectomy. Ten years ago. After nine surgeries in four months and losing my baby. *It. Is. In. My. Chart.*"

I feel like such a jerk.
It isn't this nurse's fault- heavens knows she certainly isn't the first one to refer to my possibility of being pregnant without reading my chart.
In fact, this has happened with such frequency my dear friend Joanna had a button made up for me that reads "Hi, I'm Mandolen. I had a hysterectomy. Please read my chart!".
Three years ago.
It, too, is not read.

And the leadership consultant in me reminds myself that healthcare has an **ENORMOUS** amount of #Burnout. That part, coupled with my natural inclination to just try to meet people with compassion, tells me I'm a jerk whenever I bristle in these situations.
The part of me that says "Women's care shouldn't just be about reproducing women's care. Patient care should include the emotional distress that can be caused by careless assumptions that a woman of childbearing age can bear children."

I am a woman.
I am of childbearing age.
I cannot bear children.
I am not alone.

So mostly?
In those situations I hurt for all the other women who endure these situations.

The women who keep trying and haven't yet carried the baby they've prayed for.

Those women who look inward and ask themselves the anguishing questions of "Why can't I? Why can they? What's wrong with me?"

And that's when I bristle.

That's when the jerk emerges.

Out of advocacy, not anger.

But for once, when this happened again to me this week, I didn't bristle. When I kindly explained I'd had a hysterectomy the nurse waved her hand "Oh! Well then that's easy!" I knew she meant well. And, while conflicting emotions roiled around inside of me ("**EASY?!**" I wanted to say), I sighed in resignation.

This is just how it is.

But it shouldn't be.

So I share this with you, not for me, but for the women I grieve with.

If you're in the healthcare field, please read the chart before you ask LMP or for a UA. The few seconds will save exponential heartache and consternation.

I know you're tired. I know you're overworked.

I see you.

Please see us.

If you're a patient enduring this, I am so sorry.

In those moments, my heart sits with yours.

Three

Seven years ago, in the midst of my Ph.D., I arrived at work and, upon attempting to greet a colleague, realised I could not talk. My tongue was curled, my jaw clenched, and weird straining sounds kept coming from the depths of my mouth. Having experienced muscle spasms and hand tremors in the weeks leading up to this day, I immediately called my Neurologist but was unable to convey the issue to the receptionist.

Colleagues thought I was having a stroke.

I was so scared...

Fast forward through many painful and terrifying tests and I was diagnosed with acquired torsion dystonia. The doctor informed me that within 5 years my prognosis was severe disability but that a small percentage of people beat the odds.

Time was of the essence. While the brain is plastic, if I had a chance of progress it would have to happen in that first year.

Without any playbook to work from, I fought for the life of service I dreamed of.

I chased down doctors.

I went through treatments.

I kept getting up on stages and in classrooms- deeply self-conscious of my hand tremors and how thick my accent becomes when I'm nervous.

I dealt with people claiming my illness was fake.

I moved through all of that, and arrived to today.

Today, I walked in- without the cane that helped me through those early years- to receive Botox injections in my neck, shoulder, back, and jaw.

I got a refill for the medications that calm the damaged neural pathways.

And I talked with my doctor about my upcoming appointment at Mayo Clinic.

The current hypothesis is that chronic stress has altered my genetic markers, causing a myriad of symptoms we've not been able to understand for years. I shared insight from research and the rest of my medical team.

An advocate of others who might face the challenges I've met, but also for myself. While I'm not a victim, my story of victory continues to be written.

Seven years. Two years past expectations. More up ahead, but with twisting, spastic, muscles and shaky hands, I continue to use my voice.

I continue to try to serve.

I continue.

Four

I've navigated 5-8 medical appointments every week, for two years now. Despite that, I've continued to build a career, a company, and hopefully a legacy. Seventeen years of battling Crohns, seven years of acquired torsion dystonia, a miscarriage, surgeries, cancers, years fighting PTSD, and one year of unexplained severe hypoglycemia have made me learn to be resilient. Well, that, an incredible medical team, an inherited strong work ethic, and an ingrained conviction that I have been put on this earth to use my gift and my story to serve others.

But this week, I admit, was a bit tougher.
A bit more of a challenge.
A bit more heavy lifting for me to have the energy to do my work, research, and writing.
My medical team has championed me all the while they continue to be baffled by my case, attempting to find various back-channels to cut through waiting times to Mayo Clinic.
Over and over again they say, "We don't know how you're surviving, let alone thriving!" while also validating the immense behind-the-scenes work I'm doing to keep pressing forward.
And although folks know I've endured health issues for years now, no one really gets front-row seats...except those who are listed as my ICE (In Case of Emergency) on my medical alert bracelet.

So, this is how it came to pass, that this morning cheerful flowers disrupted me from my work, sent from one of those engraved names. (It should be noted, this occurred after no less than four "Bestie Check-in" outreaches to me in the past 24-hrs!)

I've got a long list of fun projects on my "to-do" for today, but it's not the medications and specialised diet that are powering me forward: It's the inspiration of a best friend. Someone I once taught, then mentored, then befriended, then became business partners with.

She's the introvert who adopted this extrovert, and I'm all the more better for it.

If ya'll don't have a Rachelle Blitch in your life, get you one STAT.
But not her specifically...she's **MY** Bestie.

Five

I have taught 83 college courses.
My overall student evaluations average to 4.89 on a 5.0 scale. This has always meant a great deal to me- not because of my overachieving desire- but because I have only ever taught working adults. To know that I've provided value to people using their discretionary time/money/energy to better themselves is a humbling, ineffable, gift.

It's the same feeling when I get feedback from consulting clients- other working adults- who state that my training style has positively resonated with them.
MullMentum Consulting, LLC has some unbelievably kind reviews from amazing leaders and we are absolutely grateful. Today we received feedback from the IronWorkers I taught this summer. The training this year was pure MullMentum- customised and present...and a complete deviation from the norm!

This was a risk on many fronts: I was going off script and chronic, severe, hypoglycaemia had me stashing snacks all over my classroom as I never can stay in one place. That was all the more problematic as while IronWorker Week is seriously my favourite week of the year, it also exhausts me (as a professor and consultant I don't usually teach 8 hours straight for 5 days- not to mention all the fun social activities I love going to with new and old friends (and gelato...always, always, gelato)).
With Crohn's and dystonia, and now hypoglycaemia, I usually don't have a problem with short bursts of energy...but sustained?!
And. I. Was. Going. Off. Script!
Eep!
However, I knew once I got going- I'd do what I have been put on this earth to do. It's our company motto: Develop Leaders Who Develop Other Leaders.

And the feedback...ya'll.
Turns out I didn't just win at keeping my energy and engagement levels up (a common feedback praise), but that I met the goals I've had for any course I've ever taught:
1) Give them a positive experience,
2) Give them tangible tools they can readily apply to their work.
Despite all of the challenges, I lived my purpose.

Do me a favour: Lower your shoulders away from your ears.
Drop your tongue from the roof of your mouth.
Inhale through your nose, expanding your ribs and belly like an umbrella opening.
Exhale from your mouth.
Repeat, making each breath bigger, each exhale longer.
Repeat.
Repeat.
That yawn you just had?
That's your parasympathetic ("rest and digest") mode coming back online.
Now you're ready.

Epictetus asks, "How long are you going to wait before you demand the best for yourself?"
But here's the thing ya'll- it's not about demanding this from others, but rather from yourself.
When was the last time you got a win?
When was the last time you felt clear-headed and energetic?
When was the last time you got into psychological flow and worked from your heart, not realising the hours that passed by as your creativity, talent, and purpose flowed through and from you?
That's the you that you deserve.

Make sure you're demanding the best for yourself from the person who can most give that to you: **You.**

We live in a world that has scrambled our bodies, our attention, our relationships. We lose ourselves in the midst of such inauthenticity, gimmicks, and diversions. Give yourself Grace as this befalls everyone, but sadly some people never stop to realise it and thus are perpetually hijacked by inauthentic charades.

But not you.

You're taking care of the only business that really matters- the business of living out your purpose and sharing your gifts with the world.

I'm cheering you on.

Seven

"It's no measure of health to be well adjusted to a profoundly sick society."
-J. Krishnamurti

I know what you're thinking, "Wow, M, that doesn't seem very Monday Mullivation to me!" But hang tight, dear friends, because I think I'm on to something here.

We know we live in a society that is broken.
Healthcare? Broken.
Education? Broken.
Political System? So very broken.
Our work structures are fuelled by an insatiable need to "keep grinding" into perpetuity.
Our coping skills have us stress buying from Amazon, only later to remember what it was we spent our hard-earned money on whenever the packages arrive.

You'd think people would be shouting from the rooftops.
There would be artwork, literature, and songs created to turn the tide. And, so, because there's not a preponderance of these things (aside from the screaming heads on the news that most of us no longer subject ourselves to) we write folks off as being apathetic.
But what if they aren't?

What if folks are becoming immune to the broken sickness and moving forward into meaningful connections?
Meaningful adventures?
Meaningful work?
Meaningful lives?

They don't have time to be apoplectic- they have places to see, people to meet, a life to create.

Applying this to the microcosm of my life, I know my body is shackled with illness. And maybe I'm immune to it all after so many years, or maybe I just see time and life as precious, but I don't stay "well adjusted" to my illnesses. I still work, I still go on adventures, I still meet fascinating and indelible people, and I'm still pressing forward to craft a pretty rockin' life of purposeful service.

This week ahead, I hope you focus on your adventure. I hope you are unmoored from the adjustment to a "sick society" and are weaving a life of meaning.

I hope for you…so very much.

Eight

I am off on a #MulliversTravels, the significance of which I'll share later this week. But today's Mulling is about something I've shied away from most of my life: My heritage.

I have red hair.
My father had red skin.
He was Cherokee on both sides of his family, and because I did not look like him, I felt it fraudulent to embrace my Cherokee lineage. Our surname, West, derived from our ancestors being marched from their lands, was less representative of me than my elder sister's first name, Darby, the Irish surname of my mother's family of which my colouring takes after.
Darby looked like Daddy, so she got to claim the Native American genes and the Irish ones...or so I told myself.

While my father was a Christian, he retained a lot of his Cherokee traditions. I would watch with interest as he gave thanks to the spirits of the deer, turkey, or fish that fed our family.
I'd collect arrowheads with him and listen to his stories.
I learned the Cherokee nicknames and words he taught.
I cherished the dream catcher he hung in my room.
We had deep discussions about me going to college where Judge Baylor, a self-proclaimed "Indian fighter", is buried.
And, true to his heritage, my father asked for his body to be turned to ashes, not wanting the earth to be "polluted by the poison of cancer in (his) body".

But... I never felt that I am REALLY Native American if I don't look it.

So, I sat at my GDad's knee and absorbed everything about his fascinating life.

I traveled with him.

I laughed like him.

I preened when told how much I acted and looked like my Darby family.

It wasn't that I have been ashamed of being Cherokee- it's that I haven't thought I qualified.

And so, the two most influential mentors in my life, my GrandDad and Daddy, were these polar opposites to me…until they weren't.

And thus my current adventure.

One that brought them together, and one that finds me confronting the reality that feeling fraudulent for who you are is fraudulent in and of itself.

I am going west.

I am Johnny West's daughter.

I am Col. John Darby's granddaughter.

I am both.

I am me.

Nine

Three years ago my father said he wanted to visit me in Illinois, a part of the country to which he'd never been.
Only, he wished to wait until he felt better.
Cancer didn't care about his wishes.
At the time, I understood his rationale and supported his need for comfort.
In hindsight?
I think maybe it was egotistical and greedy for us to assume he'd ever have the opportunity again.

Or, at least, that's the mindset I'm adopting these days as I embrace what I've taught and trained for years: Do big things.
Do brave things.
Do the things that scare you.
Yawp barbarically over the roofs of the world.
Travel the roads less traveled.
Change the direction of your sails.
All the things.
All the sayings.
All the inspirations and aspirations…**Do it.**

Ten

Fear. It's what keeps us small.
It keeps us confined and contained.
It keeps us stuck.
"What if I get a flat tire in the middle of nowhere on my #WanderingRoadTrip?! I am not strong enough to change a tire! AND I never paid attention when Daddy tried to show me how! ...Argh, I just have to trust if it happens, I'll figure it out." This is what my friends have heard me say recently.
This is what I spoke into existence.

In the rain, cold, and wind, I found myself yesterday between cornfields with a flat. I'm really good in high-stress situations.
I am not, however, all that great when fear springs forth.
DeMandolen was raring to come unleashed as I called loved ones to help me problem-solve.
Without a plan, panic was poised.

And then Ralph out of Sioux City arrived. And in those nasty weather conditions, he found a gnarly culprit, repaired my tire, and wished me safe travels.
He wouldn't take payment.
My Daddy came out in me as I insisted.

Back on the road, hail and lightening came.
My glucose alarm kept going off as I tried to keep focused and sip sugar.
When I finally arrived to my hotel, I was exhausted.
But I thought I'd stop at the restaurant first, just to reflect on the lesson Ralph had taught me. I explained to the waitress, Kandi, I'd had a bit of an adventure and wouldn't be eating.

And it was there, as I thought about a mechanic with busted steel toes who got down in the mud and saved a stranded stranger, that Kandi returned.
Only she had brought Thomas, an inked-out chef who heard about my challenged travels and wanted to help with a blueberry cobbler cheesecake. He hoped the strawberry rose he'd carved made me feel welcomed in Nebraska.
I paid forward.

My father often showed up at restaurants in his brick-dust splattered, sweat stained, work clothes and connected with folks.
He'd see them, not their trappings.
He, the former long-haired misfit, said blue-collars like him always appreciated service-oriented workers the most. "We know the gratitude felt when someone helps."

Yesterday, my fear was reframed into faith.
I realise now I don't have to have it all planned out, I just need to be open to adventure.

And appreciate the help along the way.

Eleven

There are many reasons for my #WanderingRoadTrip but the anchor is Wounded Knee.

On December 29, 1890, nearly 300 Lakota men, women, and children were massacred by US troops. Eyewitnesses recounted of soldiers going berserk, "They fired rapidly but it seemed to me only a few seconds till there was not a living thing before us". Women with babies in their arms were found slaughtered, chased down in the snow as far as two miles away.
The horror and injustice is immeasurable.

In 2007, months before my GDad was diagnosed with cancer and over a decade before my Daddy was, I told my GDad about the movie, "Bury My Heart at Wounded Knee". He read the book and decided to go see the site. Normally his best friend would have gone with him on a road trip, but this time something unexpected happened. My father- who never took a vacation- offered to go.

Now, you should know that when my long-haired, high school drop-out, muscle-car-driving, Cherokee Daddy started dating my Momma, he wasn't quite who my Colonel grandfather would've chosen for his youngest daughter. Later, he didn't much care for all those times my Daddy's name showed up in the local jail log. But my Daddy loved history and his Native American heritage, and he wanted to go.

They drank Madeira wine, told bawdy jokes, and made memories that starred in the highlight reels of both their lives.
They wept at Wounded Knee.
The Colonel, for the wrong of the country he served.
The Cherokee, for the generational grief flowing in his genes.

They wept for what Black Elk described: "And I can see that something else died there in the bloody mud, and was buried in the blizzard. A people's dream died there. It was a beautiful dream."

It was a beautiful dream.
One I am building through my work from lessons taught by my ancestors.

So I came to find answers.
I am on a pilgrimage of honour.

Yesterday, standing in my father and grandfather's footsteps, with GDad's watch encircling my wrist of the hand that held the grains of my Daddy's ashes, I wept.
I wept for all their reasons, and for my own.
And I, too, buried a piece of my heart at Wounded Knee.

Twelve

This #WanderingRoadTrip has been a huge crucible in me exploring the Word of the Year I selected last December for 2023: *Valour.*

Valour: Honour and dignity in the face of great fear.

I've faced many fears on this trip:
Being stranded with a flat tire in the middle of nowhere.
Navigating unknown routes.
Fully experiencing the grief of my father and grandfather.
Embracing my heritage and investigating my inherent bias.
And driving in uncontrolled situations...

Two years ago I was hit by a distracted driver.
An eye witness said he saw the bottom of my car four times.
I felt each one as I called out to God to keep me safe so that my parents didn't suffer my loss.
When the chaos finally stopped, I had to be cut out of the car.
First responders couldn't believe I was alive.
Later, friends would tell me they saw it on the news.
I thought I walked away relatively unharmed...
And yet...
Sirens are the continual reminder that my body keeps the score. The sound causes my dystonia to engage as my body curls in on itself.
Sometimes, there are flashbacks.
Sometimes, it's all triggered by hitting a pothole or seeing a car come up on my right side, as I worry they, too, won't stop. The fear is a shackle I keep trying to shake loose.
I see multiple providers to help me move forward.
We work in inches, not miles.

It is hard work and we have so much more to go.

So, when Siri told me to take Wounded Knee Road the other day I didn't at first think much of it. But as I began to drive on the dirt road that had been inundated with rain, and my tires began to slide, my dystonia reacted.
The fear was extreme but no one could help me.
I had to move forward.
For ten miles, with no other vehicles or homes in sight, I talked and breathed my way through a gauntlet I'd like not to soon repeat.
I kept thinking of inches and not miles.
But an ounce more of self-confidence and progress has dropped into my currency bucket.
Inches. Not miles.

Also, once I got to the site, it was on a paved parking lot.
Off of a paved highway.
The lessons continue.

Thirteen

Whether it's the Irish or the Cherokee in me, or the fact that I find a leadership lesson in EVERY experience, I'm a big looker-outer for signs and meaning. I saw many on my #WanderingRoadTrip…only I still don't yet have answers to what they might've been trying to convey.

There were myriad reasons for my trip but the original impetus for my travels was ultimately clarity.
For those of you who've been following me for a while, you know that while I look "normal" and have seemingly endless energy, I've got some hanging question marks around my health.

For almost 18 years I've navigated Crohn's.
For 7 years I've beat the odds of a severely disabling prognosis of dystonia.
For the past two years I've battled unexplained extreme hypoglycaemia.
My heart rate, blood sugar, and blood pressure frequently live at critically low levels, yet you'd never know it by talking to me!
I have an upcoming appointment at Mayo, but this has been a long road and I'm kind of tired of all the poking and prodding- especially when I want to do fun stuff like help support folks on their leadership journey!

So, for the past few months I've asked my extensive medical team if maybe we shouldn't just accept that this is how my body was designed to operate now.
Maybe we don't need a diagnosis and all this monitoring and treatment.
Maybe I don't want to keep up with the 5-8 medical appointments I've managed each week.
Maybe, like how I've lived with Crohn's and dystonia, I can keep on keepin' on here, too.
Maybe whatever "this" is, it won't get worse.

Maybe.

My trip was an opportunity for me to not only remind myself of my strength, but to investigate how much more effort and energy I want to put toward chasing down a diagnosis, and how much I want to put toward my calling and purpose of serving others.
I'm sometimes a brat at one of these things.
Really good at the other.
I'll leave it to you to decide.

Along my wandering I saw a lot of signs that held meaning to me, but no real answers.
No penny dropped.
The journey doesn't feel complete.

And maybe that's the point of journeys anyway- they never quite end.
If we stay receptive, we keep growing with no real denouement.
Maybe there's no bow on all this tying things together.
Maybe we just have to keep looking, listening, and learning.
Maybe that's an answer in and of itself.
Maybe.

Fourteen

The line from Shawshank Redemption keeps playing in my head.
You know the one.
About the world getting itself into a big damn hurry?

It was 15 years ago this month I lost my child and the hope of having one of my own.
It was last fall when I was asked to adopt a baby, however the mother changed her mind and decided to keep her.
I guess the third time really is a charm as here in less than half an hour, I will welcome home a baby girl.

It's been a **WHIRLWIND** of the past 24 hours, ya'll! I had clients this week that had to be abruptly canceled. I never would've dreamed this could happen.
And yet...

When you open yourself up to God's plan, He opens all kinds of doors for you.
I will love this little one, keep her safe, for however long God entrusts me to be her mother.
I will enjoy every moment I get.
It is all an immeasurable gift.

Also- did I mention this all happened in the last 24 hours?!
Your girl needs *ALL* the things, *ALL* the advice, *ALL* the help, *ALL* the things.
So many things.

This is really happening, ya'll...
Whoo boy!

Fifteen

So the question everyone keeps asking: How did this come about?

I was told earlier this year "You share too much. No one needs or wants to hear your story, Mandolen." And while I can appreciate that this person felt that way, something inside me said they were **WRONG**.
God did not have me endure trials as a punishment but as a testimony.
And dangit, I live it.
I've been public about my challenges, and I have been public about the wrestling of my faith last year. I try very hard to live my values of *Transparency* and *Authenticity* (I am Johnny West's daughter, after all!).
So of course I share my story.

When I returned from my #WanderingRoadTrip last week I felt restless. I had learned many lessons but…something still felt like it was coming.
I didn't know what it could be.
I saw a road called "Opportunity Drive" and took it to see where it led…still no answers.
But something was coming, I could feel it, I just couldn't see it yet.

So, Sunday around lunchtime I took the boys for a walk and told God that He was so much better at planning my life than I am. I asked Him to do His will. I told Him whatever door He opened, I'd walk through. I immediately thought "Be careful, remember how He had you moving cross country into a house you'd not even seen a picture of and a town where you knew no one- in the throes of your dissertation?!"...

Prior to being told that no one wanted or needed to hear my story, I had shared my story.
It resonated with a special someone and when their family member became pregnant, my story was retold.

Other events happened and eventually it was decided that the baby's best interest would be to be mine.

I had no awareness that this was happening for weeks.

I got the call- out of the blue- mere hours after my prayer to God.

I was not on any foster list.

I had not had any intention of adopting after last year.

I never in my dreams thought this would happen.

But someone heard my story.

And through dark times in my life, and in others', this beautiful bright thing has occurred.

As I told Momma last night, this is by far the craziest thing I've done- in a life full of crazy things- but how can you not answer His call?

He's brought me to this, He'll bring us through it.

The family is kind and lovely, and this was not a decision they made lightly. Lots of folks worry for me as to if this will all work out to where she's mine forever, but the family seems to think so. Regardless, I cannot live in that fear. My priority is keeping her safe and myself as healthy as can be because, you know, I have her relying on me.

I've always said the #HavenInTheWoods has magical healing powers.

My dear friend Robin created that for me, I created it for my doggos, and now for Harbour.

Harbour- a safe keeping.

Christian- the mentee who taught me how to be maternal and the faith that brought her to me.

Harbour Christian is her name.

Sixteen

"This is also a win for a lot of folks who have been cheering you on for years, Mandolen. Accept their love. You matter to people and they want to support and celebrate. Don't go this alone. Ask for, and accept, help."

My best friends Rach and Robin had joked that my UPS guy would be getting a workout after the outpouring of love from everyone...

Harbour Christian and I arrived home last evening from a long day of appointments and navigating my first time taking her out of the Haven. On the drive home she slept while I thought of the new order: Change baby, make bottle, let the boys out, feed baby, feed boys, had I eaten?!

There were a few boxes in front of the door and once I got everyone settled I took care of those. Oh! But it's trash day so that meant I needed to load up my car with the garbage and head up the drive.

As I walked into the garage...

Piles, and piles, and piles of boxes and packages. Apparently the UPS driver, likely due to the rain (and because this is a small town), decided to enter my man-door and put all of them into the garage for safe keeping. I began to open some.

Sent from an old friend in HS I haven't talked with in years.

Sent from a former student.

Sent from a colleague.

Sent from an undergrad classmate.

Sent from someone I've only ever known for years on this platform but whom I love deeply.

And. I. Wept.

I couldn't even finish opening all the boxes, I didn't know where to put everything I did open (mainly because I have no clue what all these things

DO- babies are wild, ya'll!), and decided Rach gets to come over and take control of all that. She is rather bossy...which is why she's my best friend! But if ya'll could've seen me last night, exhausted and crying, standing amidst all of your love as I held out my arms trying to hold in all of the massive, overwhelming, kindness, you would know just how full my heart is.

In less than a week my entire life changed.
In some ways this has been 15 years in the making.
In others, this is all just still so very surreal.
I struggle to articulate it all.
People have said for years I'm good with words.
Heavens knows I use a lot of them.
But ya'll, I have no words.
I am grateful.
I am humbled.

I love you.

Seventeen

Woman, I see you.

For 15 years I avoided baby showers and kid's birthday parties. I changed churches when mine became heavily focused on the children's group and I was the only member in my age group without a child. I changed doctors to a provider who only treated non-child bearing women. I joked that I was a "dog mom" when people would ask- and they always asked- if I had children. And, eventually, I quit having panic attacks whenever I accidentally found myself in the baby aisle of a store, but I still kept my distance.

But I didn't tell people I was avoiding all of that. Because how do you say, "I'm happy for you but I have such an immense well of grief that if I even begin to attempt to articulate it I may not ever swim back to the top"?
I felt like a complete jerk.
I **WANTED** to be supportive. I **WANTED** to celebrate with others. I just couldn't.
Maybe that's selfish. But it felt like self preservation. And it was all I had.

I have many friends who follow me here that are continuing to find their way along the path of motherhood. And it doesn't matter if they've already experienced it, or experienced it through adoption, or still yet to experience it: a loss and grief is unique to each.

I don't have words to comfort pain that cannot be articulated, but I did want to share that I see you. My heart sits with you. And if my posts and my excitement of my newfound journey brings you any additional grief then please know I understand if you step away.
I understand if you avoid.
I understand if you need to practise self-preservation.
I understand.
And I love you.

Winter 2023

One

I'm a hybrid.
Half Irish, half Cherokee.
Scholar-Practioner.
Small in size but big in personality.

I am a nomad, living all over the map but love the security of my #HavenInTheWoods where only the local florist really knows I reside in this small town simply for the fact that no other customer buys flowers for their dogs.
I like Texas Rangers baseball but don't keep up with other teams or other sports (unless it's my UMHB Crusaders!).
I love theatre and also Will Ferrell movies.
My musical tastes are vast, ranging from Jim Croce to Cody Jinks to Cher to Gregory Alan Isakov.
I read books on weighty ancient philosophy as well as silly ones that include talking gargoyles.

All of this has often made me feel like I had to choose.
I was too messy and needed to fit into one category.
I didn't look Cherokee so I ignored that, only I wasn't fully Irish so embracing that heritage felt like I was mocking it somehow.
I wasn't publishing in top tier journals, opting for the fun work of practise, but I wasn't this metric-driven, acronym-laden, Ops person that organisations kept insisting I was supposed to be.
And, I kept getting told that my big personality and presence was a threat to others so I needed to shrink to my physical wrappings, which were shrinking from the stress of it all.

So, when that inevitably didn't work, I then tried to excel at everything!

Be the best, know the most, be someone everyone liked.
...And when that, too, inevitably didn't work, I realised I didn't have to choose one thing, and I didn't have to be everything.
I could just be.
For me.

This has been a journey, ya'll! But as I often say, I think we sometimes condemn people to past versions of themselves. We say things like "I know you!" or "You've always been X" instead of saying "Tell me about who you are now. Tell me about who you're becoming."
This next year I hope I keep becoming someone who grows wholly. Holistically.
Someone who grows in breadth and depth.
Someone who grows dynamically.
Diagonally.
Someone who bumps up against her edges and realise just how far her capacity and capabilities reach.

I hope that for you, too.

Two

I have a CEO friend who always takes 2 weeks of vacation at a time because he says he gets sick the first week. This was interesting to me as, for years now, I've noticed I always have a Crohn's flare whenever there's a break in my schedule.

It seems like when we slow down, our bodies catch-up...

I'm giving a keynote on personal awareness and self-care today. The irony is, the lessons I'll be conveying have been hard-earned on my part. For years now my medical team has told me "We don't know how you're surviving, let alone thriving!" And I figured it was just my dogged determination.

My scrappiness.

My will.

My GRIT (Girl Raised in Texas).

My father's daughter.

Plus, I kept getting rewarded for "grinding it out" and "pushing through", so why would I stop?

But next week, the Bestie and I set off for Mayo to meet with a geneticist in the hopes of understanding what my elaborate medical team has not been able to ascertain for 18 months: The cause (and cure) of chronic, unexplained, random hypoglycaemia.

But here's the catch ya'll- it never happens when I'm with a client or giving a keynote. It also didn't dip low a single time for 3 weeks after Harbour making me an instant, unexpected, mother (normally I have multiple lows a day).

I tell my medical team "I don't feel stressed" and they respond, "Of course not, this is your mode. It's how you earned your degrees and built your career. This is your normal."

Light bulbs go off for us all: *Cortisol*.

Like my CEO buddy, I'm running on stress. It doesn't **_FEEL_** like stress, but my body says otherwise.

And I don't think I'm alone.

I think a lot of folks are stress-fuelled busy-bees unaware of, or ignoring, the red flags their bodies are waving.

I don't have much advice here, as I'm still learning myself, but I wanted to share in case anyone else sees these patterns in their lives. And it's not so much a cautionary tale as I don't know that I'd have listened to myself, but let me just say: The Grind Mentality is crap.

You're not a machine.

And even if you were?

The best ones still need rest and maintenance to avoid overuse and damage.

Three

"I was distracted by the different accents." That's feedback I recently got from a client. And, despite me explaining in my presentation how I had been diagnosed with acquired torsion dystonia in the fall of 2016, during the height of my doctoral studies, and that I had to learn to re-talk and re-walk again, perhaps this individual didn't make the connection.

Truth be told, my accent is the thing I am consistently self-conscious of.
Although I've traveled and lived all over the world, my accent is from #dystonia. Often it sounds British.
Sometimes Irish.
Sometimes slurred.
Sometimes Australian.
Sometimes Texan.
Sometimes nasally as the roof of my mouth contracts.
Sometimes there's stuttering as the muscles in my jaw involuntarily clench.
Sometimes a mix of it all.
And I cannot do anything about it, as the more I get stressed, the heavier it gets.

I've been called a fraud by people who didn't understand.
I've been harassed by men who won't take my answer of "Texas" when they ask where I'm from, thinking I'm being cute.
I've had folks outright tell me they cannot understand me.
And it hurts my heart.
Because how do you tell strangers, "I have neural damage, but I beat the odds of a disabling prognosis 7 years ago and this wonky accent is a gift and a blessing."?

There were students, classmates, professors, colleagues, friends, and family who saw this all play out in real-time for months as I struggled to find answers.
They saw me walking with a cane.
They heard me struggle to speak.
They saw my hands tremble and spasm.
And because I was public at that time, when someone I taught later found themselves being diagnosed with dystonia, they told me they felt comforted because they knew if I could beat the odds, they could too, and that they weren't alone.

But each new person I meet, I have to debate telling them the truth of the origin of my speech or just going along with whatever they assume so as not to make it awkward.

I'm not ashamed of what I've overcome, but I am embarrassed by it.
However, there's not much to be done.
Some folks will understand, some will not.
I'm finally growing into a person who is okay with those odds.
After all, I've got a good track record of beating them.

Four

It is no surprise that I love music. All kinds. Totally eclectic.
And, also, no surprise that I am deeply anchored in my faith.
Raised Southern Baptist but became Episcopalian while attending a Baptist university, I've been a bit eclectic there, too.
Lastly, folks know I've faced some trials.

But I wonder if folks know about this:
In 1871, almost 30 years after my beloved (twice) alma mater and the state of Texas were founded, Horatio Spafford faced some trials. A successful business man, he had just suffered immense financial loss with the Great Chicago Fire. Then, sadly, his 4-year old son succumbed to scarlet fever.

So, Horatio decided to send his wife and four daughters to England where he would join them after righting his business affairs. Only, the ship found tragedy in the Atlantic and all four of his daughters died.

As Horatio crossed the ocean to reunite with his wife, the ship captain commemorated the place where Horatio's daughters had perished. It was then he wrote the words to the most remarkable hymn ever composed: It Is Well With My Soul.

Horatio's words: *"Whatever my lot, thou hast taught me to say, it is well, it is well, with my soul."* show immense bravery and faith.
His words, *"My sin-oh the bliss of this glorious thought! My sin-not in part but in whole, is nailed to the cross, and I bear it no more! Praise the lord, praise the lord, oh, my soul!"* conveys someone who celebrates from the trenches.

My daughter, Harbour Christian, loves when I sing to her, and while I don't have the talent of my mother who sang the Messiah, I marvel as Harbour's face lights up when I sing Horatio's words. I suspect it's not my voice, but rather the ineffable strength of soul that his indelible words impart, which resonates.

A lot of folks this time of year find themselves with trials and in the trenches.
I hope they find the bravery and faith of Horatio.
And if they cannot?
Maybe you will be the one to lighten and celebrate their load.
I believe you can.
It's what leaders do.

Five

I'd like to tell you about my friend, USMC Sgt. Justin Monk.

Childhood friends, he was an all-star athlete and me the debate captain. After graduation I went to college and he took the call to serve.
Serving in Operation Whalers and taking enemy fire that immediately wounded his fellow Marines, Justin carried the wounded up the mountain, saving many lives that day.

When he retired, Justin went to college to become an ER nurse. Led strongly by his faith, he comforted many scared souls. He married a high school friend and had four beautiful children. We didn't really interact much, you know, but there was once this disagreement...
On Facebook.
About politics.

In early 2019, I heard that Justin had rare tumors in his brain and spine.
So, knowing my way around the medical world, I offered help.
And, as such, it just so happened that after discovering the hospital had made an egregious mistake, I made some phone calls that ensured the Chief Medical Officer personally oversaw Justin's case.
Having done what I could, I went back to dealing with my own health issues. But then I got a call from a friend telling me something Justin had said which really bothered me: "I can't believe she's helping me. I thought she was mad at me over that politics stuff on Facebook."

My buddy thought I wouldn't help because of a lame, one-dimensional, social media back-and-forth of which I still cannot recall the details.
That hurt my heart, ya'll.
A lot.

So, I made a prayer quilt, packed up my favourite chemo supplies, and I headed down to Texas.

But before I did, I made sure to get matching shirts (mine with a donkey and his with an elephant) for my new Chemo Twin.

When I surprised him in his hospital room that day, I announced, "I heard there's someone in here who wants to talk about politics!"

Justin reached for my hand and began to cry.

'We ain't talkin' politics!' he said as we both wiped tears away.

I told him I had changed my chemo days to match his.

He wasn't fighting alone.

We had a beautiful visit and as I got ready to leave, I promised him to a foot race the next time I saw him. This was silly as Justin was an incredible runner but wasn't able to walk well due to the tumors, and I was nearing being on a feeding tube.

But we were in the trenches, my buddy and I, and we were going to fight forward.

We never did get that race, but Justin beat the cancer and ran in his own #MonkStrong benefit 5K.

Our entire hometown poured out support.

It was nothing less than he deserved.

The cancer came back.

And a year ago today, my friend took his last breath.

This is probably where it feels natural to tell you that the world got darker when Justin Lee Monk left…but it didn't.

Remarkably, unexpectedly, it didn't.

Because my friend had shown so much immense light during his lifetime that there are innumerable pinpoints of goodness all over this world today because of who he was.

I miss my friend. I miss him picking on me. I hurt for his amazing family and all who loved him.

But I'm really, really, glad he was here.
Because this world, and so many people's faith, has been bettered by him.

And I hope folks vote.
I hope we'll honour people like my friend Justin, who fought for this country and the freedoms which were as hard to win as his battle against cancer.
My friend who cancelled out my vote, yet we both got excited to do it.
Both were honoured to do it.

Politics isn't a four-letter word, ya'll.
It's uniquely personal to each person, so I understand the emotionality of it.
But my goodness, it sure as heck isn't something that should make us so vile and vitriolic that a dying man would be surprised his old friend would offer help when he needed it.
We stand on the shoulders and in the shadows of giants.
Let's see that we honour them well.

Six

I didn't like what my doctor had to say, so I ghosted her. For three weeks. Turns out, she's even more stubborn than I am.

Yesterday started the 12th annual Crohns and Colitis Awareness Week. Eighteen years ago, I was diagnosed with severe Crohn's disease, a condition of which I'd never even heard about let alone knew of someone who had it. In those 18 years, a lot has happened.

I've had 23 scopes.
Surgeries.
Countless appointments.
Infusions.
Injections.
So very many pills.
Acquired torsion dystonia (presumably from my meds).
Skin cancer (presumably from my meds).
Trips to Mayo Clinic.
Feeding tubes.

Painful and invasive treatments.
I lost a baby.
I've lost weight.
I've lost my toenails.
I've lost my hair (Seriously, ya'll. Literal insult to injury. It's not vanity, it's sanity!).

In 18 years I've earned multiple advanced degrees.
Won awards.
Built a career.

Travelled.
Founded a company.
Published a book.
Became a Momma (Squee! I still cannot believe it!)!

However, an unexpected thing I've experienced was what my ghosted doctor diagnosed me with two years ago: An eating disorder.

Despite having seen the best gastroenterologists in the world, and despite all my attempts to be a good patient in researching my own complex case, I never once came across info that is extremely prevalent to #MeAndMyCrohnies.
I didn't know it wasn't normal to only eat once a week.

I didn't know it wasn't normal to wake up several hours early to ensure you weren't symptomatic at work.
I just thought I was doing what was necessary for me to have a career while battling a chronic disease.
I thought I was being successful.
I didn't know that 93% of folks with Crohn's or UC have disordered eating.
I didn't know.
And so when my doctor told me, I was ticked.
First at her.
Then at all the others who never told me.
Then at myself.

I was angry because I've come so far in my growth to not have had awareness.
I literally tell everyone self-reflection is the biggest tool for growth and yet here I was so on brand with "physician, heal thyself!"
I was angry because although my eating disorder originated from physical limitations, it had begun to be exacerbated by my behaviours.
And, ya'll, I was angry because despite all my work, there was still so much more to do.

As my case is complex, for two years I've been putting in the work.
No less than 5 appointments each week.
Nutritionists.
Gastro Psychologists.
Two different GI doctors.
Physical therapy.
Somatic therapy.
Neurologist.
Endocrinologist.
Cardiologist.
Cognitive therapy.
It all helps, immensely.

But you know what helped the most? That ghosted doctor who didn't give up on me. Who, from just one visit (in which I got angry), she saw something in me and believed I could fight forward.
What an indelible gift.
It is my hope that by sharing my story, I help someone else believe they, too, can fight forward.

See ya'll #InTheArena.

Seven

Survivor's Guilt. We see this a lot in the military, folks who have endured trauma, folks who remain after layoffs.
It's not something we particularly talk about.

"Why me?" These survivors ask. "Why did it happen to them and not me?"
And often they are (well-meaning but unhelpfully) told: Just be grateful.

And the converse, the "Why me?" asked when bad luck has befallen someone is equally met with an: Others have it worse.

Oh, the ways in which we dismiss these complex feelings.
The ways in which we dismiss having to dig into questions we don't yet have answers for.
The ways in which we dismiss each other- and ourselves.

The first time I arrived at Mayo Clinic in 2021 I stepped off into a hallway and wept. My father and childhood friend Justin were battling terminal cancer back in Texas, and I was getting to see the best doctors in the country for GI issues that had led to chronic malnourishment.
It seemed…unbalanced.
Muscle-bound scrappers, these two men were far stronger than I was.
I had "tummy troubles".
I didn't understand.
I didn't know what to do with the complexity of gratitude and guilt swirling around me.

But I **WAS** humbled.
I was honoured.
I was grateful.

I knew how many times I kept falling through the cracks, being passed off to this specialist or another, all the misdiagnoses.

I knew I had a doctor back in Illinois who believed in me enough to tell me, "My ego is big, but not so big I won't put your health first. Your case is beyond what I can help with. We have to get you to Mayo."

So I absolutely felt such gratitude.

I also felt guilty.

That first day, as I was composing myself, I saw a sign for the Mayo Clinic store and directed myself that way. Arriving, there was a hoodie in the window which read, *"Diagnosis Optimism"*.

I bought it.

Most people looking at it would think it means I have optimism about my own case (I do).

But in that moment I had optimism that I'd one day understand all this complexity.

I still have that hope.

Those two brave men are passed now.

And I sit here, once again at Mayo, with my coffee, watching optimism and hope walk by my window.

I wonder the stories these people have.

I wonder of the Grace they give themselves when guilt arrives.

I wonder if, as I go about my appointments today I can make any of their lives a little brighter. A little more optimistic.

Maybe not in the way my hoodie reads.

But in the way that one day we'll understand.

Eight

So many discussions about mental health focus on self-care items that aren't my brand. I don't like massages. If you give me a day off I'll fill it with other work. Physical challenges aren't my jam. But I still did these things because it's what I was "supposed" to do, right? I had never seen adults healthfully self-regulate after a bad day.
So I had no model.
The universal checkboxes were it.

And when I was relearning to walk and talk in 2019 due to dystonia I received an unexpected gift of a prayer quilt. It was made for me by strangers I will likely never meet. The overwhelming humbleness of that act is ineffable. There simply are no words.

So, I began to embrace the power of a blanket.
As others I loved fought their own health battles, I started gifting prayer quilts and cosy blankets. This gave me a feeling of agency in trying to convey words I didn't have. "I'm sending you safety, rest, comfort, warmth, healing, and love." Oftentimes there were my favourite ginger chews thrown in to combat the chemo nausea or some soup to nourish. Or maybe facial masks, candles, aromatherapy, quirky cards. I've sent bouquets of specific flowers which symbolise healing, health, and comfort.
These were all tangibles to try to convey the intangible.

And that's one of the things I think we really get wrong in our discussions of "self-care" or the non-existence of "work/life balance". We assume we know what comforts another. In our well-meaning attempts, we forget to speak in the currency of the other person.

What is **YOUR** brand of comfort? For me it's blankets, my pups, a delicious cuppa, hugs, gelato, climbing into clean bedsheets after a hot shower. It's traveling and speaking to strangers in passing. It's the sounds of chatter at small baseball fields. Losing hours in a tucked away bookstore. Flowing water. Good music.

But mine may not be yours, and you could try them all and realise none of it helped. Until you know **YOUR** brand, I don't think we start to move the needle with this discussion.
Find your brand.
Find you.

Nine

I woke up in my snow-globe hidden away in the woods.
My half-mile drive still not plowed.
Wifi still out.
My grandfather clocks ticking...

There's a ton I need to get done. A veritable scroll of "to dos" that truly will not complete themselves. But for a bit I'm just going to sit.

Because in the past 90 days I have: Navigated my way on a 7-state #WanderingRoadTrip, become a solo mother overnight (although the Bestie is convinced she's considered a parental unit), given a dozen keynotes, taught graduate courses, kept the #HoundAndTerrier fed and groomed, become an even more interesting guinea pig to Mayo, been headhunted from employers across the country, battled a never-ending head cold and cough that has now become one with my spirit, and survived a visit from my mother.

Now, note this, dear friends- I don't share this as a laundry list to tell you how busy I am. I share this to tell you I didn't think I could do it. Any of it. Well, except for maybe managing the doggos...

I sat on the side of the road, between two cornfields in the freezing rain in nowhere Nebraska, with a flat tire. My heart racing with my biggest fear (aside from aliens- that's a different story) in front of me, I jammed up. Until I didn't.

That first night holding my daughter as various people unloaded baby things all throughout my Haven, I felt ice grip my heart as it moved into my throat. And then, all of the sudden, I was a Momma.

Watching the Mayo team's face light up as a new, rare, white whale research project sat in front of them- me- I felt myself want to retreat.
But I walked down the stairs, got poked six times, and had my DNA sent off to be studied and cryogenically frozen for further research.

My mom? Ya'll, let's just say all the things I didn't do is why I did!

I have one of those strangely blessed but also outrageously insane, death-defying, almost absurdly comical, lives that people keep telling me should be a book. Or a movie. Or a ballad sung by the eternally amazing Cher (please let it be this option!). And I honestly have a hard time telling it in chronological structure these days.
I forget all the turns and loops.
I definitely forget all the successes.
Which means I forget to stop and collect my wins. And that is a shame as I often tell folks to ensure they take count of their wins each day.
Physician, heal thyself...

In the past three months, I've had some ***MIGHTY*** wins, ya'll.
So, just for a bit, I sit.

Ten

"Aren't you going to eat?"
"You don't like my cooking?"
"Can't you just try...?"

Even after being misdiagnosed with gastroparesis and celiac, diagnosed with Crohn's, and being put on a feeding tube, I still fielded these questions every family gathering. My loved ones meant well, but the perennial people-pleaser in me felt a lot of shame for not adhering to their expectations. After far too many instances of giving in and subsequently getting sick, I began to bring my ubiquitous Boost with me to holidays. And, when even that wasn't enough to stop the comments and questions, and I'd grown tired of the chalky drink, I just quit going.

Now, there's a whole elaborate and boring tale here that finds me currently planning with my dietician our strategy if Mayo's recommendation of resuming tube feeding is carried out. But in the middle of it, there was a lot of stress and drama.

And it wasn't just because my GI system is an absolute disaster.

These couple of days a lot of folks are going to say things like, "I shouldn't eat this but..." or "I'll start my diet next week." Probably they'll comment on someone's appearance or their own. This all makes sense because- just like in all those business books we read- we're "fed" the wrong information.

We're told if we do X, Y will occur.
We're told there's a magic strategy.
We're told *THIS* method is the one to save us for good.

And we're told if we are anything other than what that unreal end result looks like, then we're just not trying hard enough.

Diet culture is complete rubbish.
Extreme exercise is abusive.
And there is no one-size-fits all because my 6'6 400lb buddy and I can eat and work out the same and still have vastly different health and body shapes.

But we don't talk about that truth- in our personal lives or in our business.

There. Is. No. Universal. Truth. Here. But. This:
Everything is situational.
Everything is multivariate.
And everything- constantly- is changing.

So enjoy your holiday meal, or don't, completely shame-free.
Because who you are and how you operate isn't by someone else's playbook.
You were uniquely made.
You are constantly changing.
You will not pass this way again.
Celebrate it.

Eleven

It was a green dress.
One that I really loved for the way it complemented my hair.
For the way it represented my Daddy's favourite colour.

I had no reason to expect anything bad would happen to me.
No reason not to trust the person I went for drinks with.
After all, I'd had drinks with him before.
Both my husband and I had, actually.
And of course, he was well known.
Powerful.
Connected.
So certainly nothing bad would happen.

But it did.

I'm not sure what surprised me at first.
The fact that it happened.
That it happened so quickly.

That the bobby pins holding my hair up dug into my scalp as he held the back of my head, preventing me from moving away from his assault.
That my entire skin crawled as his other hand crawled all over my body-violating me more.
That all of this was happening in a public place.
Or the realisation that if I used the self-protection strategies my Daddy taught me, that I would be ruining my career.

I type this and I shiver.
Repulsed by what happened to me.

Repulsed by my inaction.
Repulsed that I valued my career over my own body and safety.

I don't remember how I finally got him to stop.
I just remember thinking I had to be as calm as possible to get out of there without angering him.
He suggested we go back to his office. Or mine.
Staring straight ahead I said I needed to leave. It was late.

"You know, Mandolen, a lot of people could be hurt if you say anything about this."
He said other things in that vein.
Something about his wife.
Something about his reputation.
Something about mine.
And it all sounded like it was coming through a shroud of water. Garbled and muffled.

Rigid, I stood up to leave.
He followed me to my car.
He made one more threat before walking away.
As soon as he was gone, I fell to my knees and vomited all over my green dress.
The green dress I had loved but threw away as quickly as I could.
Getting into my car, I called a friend.

They couldn't even understand me through the tears, screams, and gagging.

He kept calling me.
Texting me.
Trying to corner me.
I just wanted it all to go away.

He wouldn't let it.
So when I finally sent a message that what he did was wrong and to not contact me again, he got one last attack in, "It was intensely mutual, Mandolen."

I know all about narcissistic gaslighting.
I know about people who have wounds in themselves and thus wound others.
I know a great deal about extending compassion for others despite their messiness.
I do not know how to extend any compassion for him.

I later heard about other women he had done it to.
I didn't blame them for not going public.
I never did.

And when a friend asked me why?
"Because I haven't overcome all the things in my life to allow him to ruin my ability to help others. Because it will, you know. It'll be a he said/she said and I'll never be believed. And I'm not willing to have my identity, my value, my ***purpose*** changed because of him. He doesn't get to rewrite my story."

I don't know if I made the right decision.
It's one I still struggle with.
It's taken me years to tell others and even now, I am nauseous, horrified, and crying as I write.
Not because he holds anything over me- he doesn't.
But because of what I did to myself.

After this happened, I begged friends to answer one question: ***"What is it about me that made him think it was okay to do that?"***

Spring 2024

One

I think for many of us the hardest thing to do is to know when to step off and when to step into.
It's all a risk.
And, loss aversion theory tells us that we feel a loss of something 3x more powerfully than we feel the gain of something.
So...risk seems reckless, right?

I'm getting a feeding tube.
Again.
And, while this is not an imminent issue and I have time to continue to drag my petulant small-girl-child feet, it's a decision I have to make before I won't have a choice.
Because of myriad factors, my nutritional intake is suffering, and it has been since fall of 2019 when I was first put on a feeding tube. When spring came and whispers of a pandemic began, I got nervous and asked to have the tube removed. We all knew we hadn't solved the issue that led me to needing the tube to begin with.

So, between then and now, it's been an incredibly messy road. Lots of hard work as I subjected myself to multiple appointments each week with various doctors, therapies, and dieticians. Lots of wrangling with unhealthy coping skills I had acquired (avoiding eating, workaholism). And while we have made progress, the reality is I teeter just above the line of "being sick enough".

Thus, my doctors ask "How much longer?" And the truth of it all is that a feeding tube is fairly benign- except for that whole part where I'll temporarily have a tube up my nose and snaked down into my small intestine.
Which is not neat.

And, you know, a tube and a vent in my belly.
Also not neat.
But, being able to no longer constantly worry about my nutrition, or to have to set timers and carry Mandolen-approved snacks everywhere just to ensure I'm getting enough intake each day?
Well , ya'll, that sounds nice.
That is neat.

So, I'm sitting with this decision a bit more. It's not yet a burning platform, but the funny thing about acceptance is it comes like one of those moving walkways in the airport: If you step on it, it'll meet you and carry you forward.

I think for many of us the hardest thing to do is to know when to step off and when to step into.
It is all a risk.
And yet you're the bet to take.
Whatever it is that brings you peace, that brings you safety, that brings you calm and confident stability- that's not so much a risk, then, is it?

Two

It is easier to find men who will volunteer to die, than to find those who are willing to endure pain with patience.
That's what Julius Caesar claimed, and you know, I think he was right.

People have been talking a lot to me about patience lately and, quite frankly, I'm growing a bit tired.
A wee scratchy.
A midge rankled.

Full transparency, I have no idea what my life looks like in six months.
None.
Nada.
Zilch.

My (foster) motherhood.
My career.
My geography.
My nutrition.
Not. A. Clue.

Because four months ago I decided to relinquish my #GinjaNinja ways of directing my life and instead let God illuminate my path forward. That led to all kinds of unexpected opportunities and situations that are still playing out today.

Right about the time I became an unexpected overnight mother, I was getting recruited for multiple jobs across the country.
I also started becoming an even more rare and exceptional lab rat for medical research.

While I quite like being in control of situations, I like God's plans for my life a lot better.
I'm letting Him lead, and so far, He's keeping me on my toes.
It's about five different plates spinning in the air.
Has been for months.
No idea when a denouement will arrive.

Now, for someone who had her life planned out at 12, or, who five months ago was considering moving across the globe, I'm...actually, surprisingly, kinda bored.
Sure, I've got an incredibly busy schedule but I keep feeling like all this energy is supposed to be going **TOWARD** something, not just taking care of the present as I cartoonishly suspend in this waiting space.

Friends and family are a bit freaked out.
"Aren't you anxious?" They ask-having, you know, met me.
'...Nah...not really. I figure it'll happen when it's supposed to.'
"What will?"
'Whatever it is.'
They swallow their tongue.
This is not the Mandolen they know.

That Mandolen, ya'll, she had colour-coded daily planners, thick project files with contingencies, and personal strategic plans for the next 1, 3, 5, and 10 years.
She also had a lot of anxiety.
And maladaptive coping skills.
And froze up when plans didn't go as intended.
She didn't know how to fail forward, faster.
She certainly didn't know how to embrace the unknown.

The saying is that a bird on a branch doesn't concern itself with the strength of the branch.
That's not where its trust lies.
Its trust, my friends, is in its wings.

I think ol' Jules was right- it **IS** hard to endure pain with patience.
So many don't.
And maybe that's why folks feel the need to keep giving me unsolicited advice about being patient.
But I'm learning it's a little easier to hang with it all when I know I can fly as I wait to meet that next branch.

Three

I'm going to regret telling ya'll this but, well, here I'm off to share with you my greatest fear.
A-things.
Okay, sure, that's not what other people call them but that's the term I use because my unreasonable phobia is so significant that I cannot bring myself to utter their actual name.
Aliens.

So when I was a wee Mandolen I was obsessed with science. Instead of toys, I collected microscopes and telescopes. I also read every book and watched every movie about outer space. Which included the scariest movie ever made: Fire in the Sky.

I was too young to watch this supposedly true story about a logger getting abducted by a-things but so insistent was I that I NEEDED to see it, my parents finally capitulated.
Halfway through I realised I was absolutely not having a good time.
I don't remember the rest, but I do recall the severe night terrors I had for years thereafter.
And how I refused to stay the night at my friends' houses because they lived in the country (where folks apparently get beamed up).

I also distinctly remember a scene from the movie with Travis Tritt sitting around a campfire.
I've recently learned Tritt is not in that movie.
Nor is anyone else who looks even remotely like him.
Definitely something my therapist and I are unpacking...

And my fear was never assuaged as my parents delighted in my terror.

My father snuck into my bedroom at night in a glow-in-the-dark a-thing mask, and a family of Santa a-things appeared on the front lawn at Christmas.

Look, I'm not saying my aversion is rational.
I'm just saying if they do exist, I want zero part of it.
So, why am I telling you this?
Well, because the entire reason I was obsessed with science was because my mother told me that she could see me being a scientist one day.
I was little, so "scientist" sounded like "scion test" and it seemed cool, ya'll!
I didn't know what all it entailed, but my mother could see it for me and so all the sudden, I could too.

I carried that (and the phobia) with me all through undergrad where I was pre-med, but organic chemistry and a professor who took to uninvitedly calling me Mandy ruined that.
And then I never really considered myself a "Management Scientist", although, one could argue that Ops Leaders are exactly that.

But as I pursued my doctorate in change my classmates and I bandied around the idea of a Change Scientist. We weren't just Agents or Leaders- we were observing, experimenting, controlling, producing, and improving change. We danced between the art and the science; the practice and the scholastic study.

Today I'm not the scientist I thought I'd be when my mother said that strange word. But I'm the one she envisioned.
Because she didn't have a target for me, just the goal of possibility.
And somehow, along the way, I found my niche.
All because she saw something I didn't yet see.
So maybe a-things aren't real.
I've never spied one.
But I'm now, more than ever, convinced of the possibility of things not yet seen.

Four

"I have a pretty substantive drinking problem. I think it makes me more relatable to my patients."

"Do you think you have Stiff Person Disease?"
Me, looking at the unknown number on my phone, 'Who is this?'
"Dr. X. I just heard about it on the BBC. Celine Dion has it. Do you think you do?"
'...You're my doctor! Do **YOU** think I do?!'

"I don't know how to help you. But don't worry, 90% of the time I have no clue with you."
"You smell nice. That's not something I get to often say in my line of work."
"I know what's wrong with you- you don't have a stable man in your life. Get you one of those, or a lobotomy, and then all your problems will resolve."

This is the rapport I have built with my doctors over the years.
"Doctor to doctor..." they start out conversations.
I have to remind them I'm not that kind of doctor.
And, for years now, they've told me they don't know how I continue to keep up with my quality of life.
Or my heavy workload.

Because here are the other convos we have:
'I can't worry about needing to run to the restroom in the middle of a lecture. Or my glucose monitor going off in a keynote. Or my muscles contracting during a talk.'

And the one I'll have with my doctor tonight: 'Talk me through this. How do I hide the feeding tube when I'm up on stage? Will the ostomy bag make

noises while I'm talking with clients? Will this finally solve the random and continual blood sugar crashes?'
And the big one: 'What is our confidence level that this will actually work? Do we think it will or is it that we have no other option left?'

But what I'm really asking is: 'How do I keep hiding the worst parts of all this to keep my dignity?'

For years people have told me "But you don't look sick."
I know.
Because I have this medical team.
Medications.
Tools.
Strategies.
I wake up hours before I need to, consume very little, know where the nearest restroom is, and carry extra clothes, just to accommodate the worst parts of the Crohn's.
I talk through muscle contractions as my dystonia shifts my speech and gait, or I continually move my hands so no one notices the tremors.
I carry glucose gels for the hypoglycaemia.
I breathe through and fight back tears and dystonia when emergency sirens scream past.

Because looking sick isn't "professional".
It's not what a consultant does.
It's not pleasant to talk about these things.

It's not pleasant to live with them.

I don't know what my life will look like with a j-tube and an ostomy. But I suspect it'll be better. Less anguish debating over which food would satisfy my hunger while being kind to my failing digestive system. Possibly less

glucose alarms going off throughout the night as I roll over and choke down cornstarch mixed with water.
But the self-confidence?
The composure?
The dignity?
Yeah...ya'll...that's gonna take me a bit.

I'm inspired by those who've come before me.
I am hopeful.
I am growing.

Five

It's hard for me to remember. Or to narrate it all chronologically. I keep telling folks that sometimes it feels like a movie, or that it all happened to someone else.

Here's my best attempt to capture some of it:

1998: Told I'd never have children. Diagnosed with my first cancer (we blessedly caught it early, as we have the 12 that have come since).

2006: Diagnosed with severe Crohn's disease.

2008: A newlywed, we found out we were expecting! ...And then we lost him. Years of procedures, pain, and treatments.

2012: Completed my MBA as Outstanding Student of the Year.

2013: Nine surgeries in four months, the 8th horrifically traumatic, resulted in a hysterectomy. My husband moved out.

2015: Began Ph.D.

2016: Diagnosed with acquired torsion dystonia and functional dystonia. Told I'd be severely disabled in 5 years. Fought through learning to walk and talk again.

2017: Hospitalised a total of 22 days.

2018: Completed Ph.D. with 4.0 and as Outstanding Student of the Year.

2019: Faculty of the Year. Two promotions. Feeding tube. Daddy diagnosed with cancer.

2020: Covid. Employee of the Year. Hospitalised a total of 15 days.

2021: Less than 24 hours after being released from the hospital where I was pumped full of so much fluid I gained 31 lbs in 5 days, a distracted driver ran a stop sign. I rolled 4 times and was cut out of my car. Cut out of my clothes. Two weeks later a Mayo visit for nutritional issues.

2022: 40 Under 40. Daddy died. Severely malnourished, chronic hypoglycaemia began. Family member asked me to adopt their child. Months after preparing, they decided to keep the baby.

2023: Best Motivational Speaker. 40 Under 40 (again). I decided to become an entrepreneur full-time. Mayo suspects extremely rare (<40 cases) genetic disorder (DNA sequencing underway). I got a random call and asked to become a mom to a newborn. Less than 24 hours later, Harbour was in my arms.

Throughout, many doctors, pills, infusions, injections, treatments, grief.
Throughout, I kept working and excelling professionally.
Throughout, I fought forward. Not always prettily. Not always gracefully. Not always on my feet.
Throughout, I believed that there was a purpose to it all.

Harbour Christian.
I was **MADE** for this, ya'll. I was made for her. I was made to be her Momma. All the trials. All the tears. All the pain.
She is my reward.

As I prayed to God this morning I said, "Had I known…all the beauty you would bring me from those ashes…I stand in awe. I stand in humility. I stand in honour.
Thank you.
Merci.
Merci beaucoup.
Je suis reconnaissant."

Never, never- ***NEVER*** - give up hope, ya'll.

Six

In 2007, a year before I lost my son, #BereavedMothersDay was founded for the first Sunday in May. Unlike the traditional Mother's Day which is observed on various dates across the globe, this specific day is recognised internationally.

For 15 years I've honoured it in my own way and braced myself for the upcoming US celebration.

The one where I didn't fit.

I made a mistake that first year after my loss and went to a restaurant for lunch. The well meaning waiter wished me a Happy Mother's Day and I froze. Looking around me I saw signs and placards celebrating Mothers.

I felt like a terrible person.

I still had my mother to celebrate.

Grandmothers, and my sister, too.

But all I could feel was a massive emptiness and a loss so profound that I still do not have words.

So, every year after, I hid.

I couldn't even watch tv as commercials told me to "celebrate Mom" and my beloved Rangers sported pink as they did various things to honour theirs.

And, once again, I felt terrible.

I wanted to support other women. I wanted to celebrate the women in my life.

I just couldn't get past the gaping maw inside me that- if I stopped and sat with it long enough- would engulf me so much that I lost my breath.

Last year I commissioned an art piece from my friend Alex. We looked at her other work for inspiration.

"What about a man lifting you up out of a boat?"
'No, Alex.'
"What about you floating through the sky with a family trailing down off of you?"
'No, Alex. There's no one. Just me.'

For weeks now I've timidly told friends that next week will be the first time I get to celebrate Mother's Day.
The first time in 15 years where I won't hide.
And while, in the eyes of some my role as a foster mom is merely temporary, my heart tells me I am absolutely a mother.
That I do belong.

Yet I suppose that's the duality of life I've been missing all this time.
I only had love and loss.
Not love, loss, and life.
And after the painful sterilising surgeries, I had hurt.
Not hurt, hope, and healing.

I have no idea what this time for me next year may look like.
I may be preparing for my first celebration as an official, "real", mother.
It may be a time of mourning a different kind of loss of having raised a child who returned back to her bio family.
I don't know.

But I do know that the grief I carry today for my little one who didn't stay, will always be with me.
I know that the joy I celebrate next week- even in this amorphous and unknown space- will be important for me to experience.
If next week is the only time in my life I get to feel like I belong, then I will absorb as much as I can.

I cannot tell you what it feels like to lose a child.
I can detail it superficially. I can tell the facts.
But the feelings?
I don't have words for them.
But I do know that for 15 years I've lived part of the story.
And I so deeply- so viscerally- so lovingly, hope that all the women recognised today can feel all the parts.
And that they, too, feel like they belong.

Seven

The lyrical poet Bono once sang about being stuck in a moment that you couldn't get out of.
So I'm gonna level with ya'll: I'm juggling a lot of stress.
Now, this normally is my operating mode, right? I've never NOT had a ton of plates spinning simultaneously.
And yet…

One of my doctor's told me "I didn't think you could possibly be under more stress than you were last year, and yet here we are."

And it's not like I'm not using my own tools, ya'll. I totally am! But there's only so much diaphragmatic breathing, journaling, therapy, somatic shaking, and walks in the woods can do.
The stress I'm under is from forces which are outside my Circle of Control.
This is on top of my normal operating stress (the kind I like).

On top of my multivariate health-related stress (the kind I wish would just frickin' improve already).

Despite my continued efforts, I'm hanging with Bono's moment.
I am vulnerable and trusting.
And on my word, if one more person tells me to have patience or lean into my faith I'm going to use one of my constant prayers to ask God to make their playlist permanently get stuck on 'My Sharona'.

Do I keep taking on more clients and stay on the path of being an entrepreneur?
Do I follow the breadcrumbs back to teaching full time? Or back to administration?

Do I take the job offers back in corporate?
Do I set up Harbour's nursery if I don't know if I'll get to adopt her?
Do I do it anyway, and if she's not a part of my life forever then just trust myself to be resilient enough to deal with- once again- dismantling a nursery for a child of which I'm no longer a mother?
Do I listen to the doctors and hold off on the feeding tube until things settle down as they worry all this stress renders us unable to verify its effectiveness?
Do I regress back to a liquid diet, after fighting **SO** hard for the past three years where I've finally advanced to fancy meals such as pudding cups and tuna pouches?

These are the behind-behind-the-scenes, ya'll.
I usually am transparent in this space but these are the questions I'm asking my closest circle.
So why do I share it here?
Because folks need to know that while we have a lot of agency to "change our environment", sometimes we have to hang out in Bono's moment.
But it's just that- a moment.
Sometimes, I admit, an agonisingly long one.

I don't have all the answers, friends.
In these moments I can do all the self-care in the world, I can trust my faith and try to grow in this space, and...*all the things*...but until one of the logs damming up my energy flow breaks free, I'm going to jam up.

So, if any of this speaks to you and the place you're in right now, know you're not alone.
I'm here, being my quirky self, and together we'll keep company.
We'll get past the jam.
Past the moment.
But until then, I'll be stuck in the middle with you.
At least we'll have a good soundtrack.

Eight

It's not vanity, it's sanity.

I was nine when I lost my hair for the first time. My concerned mother took me to the family doctor as multiple tests were conducted to try to ascertain the cause. Lacking any explanation I remember staring in horror at the shiny, bald, dome of our doctor as he told my mother, "I personally find thinning hair attractive."

The best anyone could deduce was that anytime I had a fever, my hair would turn brittle and much of it would fall out.
We didn't know about Crohn's then.

So, my mother took me to a new hairstylist, who apparently knew very little about hair texture, to have my hair cut short. What would've been a nice style on someone with straight hair looked like Medusa with my curls.
Instead of a pageboy, I looked like a boy.

And when my hair began to grow back it was a different colour and texture. My father, who had worn his hair long for decades, showed me how to braid it.
And, then, it fell out again.
And again.
And again.

Each time I would cry for weeks, feeling as if it was literal insult to injury.
My self-esteem plummeted.
After I was diagnosed with Crohn's, I lost my hair along with 40lbs and all colouring in my skin. I looked like one of those dancing Zombies in "Thriller". And I caught myself looking in the mirror and saying, "Och, you look sick."
A giant red stop sign appeared in my mind's eye!

Nope, we weren't going to do that.
We weren't going to literally speak that negativity into my life.

Right then I remembered my Nana's motto, "There's nothing that good heels, perfume, and pearls cannot fix" and I went to find the "good" jewellery she had given me.

Little by little, I made progress forward.
I started wearing the "good" perfume on just normal days.
I wore heels- **AND** learned to walk in them!
I bought dresses that were easier to wear and reduced the drama associated with trying to find clothes that fit during a Crohn's flare or prednisone stint.
And, when my hair fell out again, I got hand-tied hair extensions.

People today make uninvited comments on my appearance.
And they have no understanding that what the world sees is absolutely irrelevant to what I see whenever I look in the mirror.
Because I don't see the trappings of society's expectations.
I see me.

And I don't see a sick woman anymore.
I know she is, but I don't see that in her.
Instead, I see someone who reframed negative stories she was telling herself.
I see a woman who found a way, through adversity beyond her control, to control her own ability to protect her peace, her self-esteem, her own value of self.
I see a woman who believes others can do the same.

It's not vanity.
It's sanity.

Nine

"Mandolen's light is always the last one on at night." That's what a colleague said when they nominated me for an accolade.
Such were the things I was rewarded for.

People saw the coffee-carrying, high-energy, upbeat #GinjaNinja hitting metrics and climbing the organisational hierarchy. They knew I was sick- it wasn't something I hid- but, well, they didn't *KNOW*.

"Ice Queen...damaged goods..." those words floated up to me as I sat on the stairs, hugging my knees to my chest, in the house we had bought for a son that was never born. A week prior to finding out I was pregnant, still in the first year of our marriage, my husband came home and said, "It's too hard being married to a sick woman. As a paramedic/firefighter I work with sick people all day. I don't want to come home to one."
I understood.
I was the breadwinner, and all that effort I was expending to keep the lights on and keep energised at work meant I was completely drained once I crossed the threshold.
He got the leftovers.
It wasn't enough.

But, that following week, after the pink lines appeared and I nervously told him, he was thrilled.
All he'd ever wanted to be was a father, he said.
The prior week's announcement was seemingly forgotten.
So, we bought a new house.
A new car.
The heartbeat wasn't there.

But now we had this new house.
This new life.
So, we kept on.
I enrolled in my MBA.
I climbed the company ladder.
I took on side jobs.
I won awards.

And the surgeries came.
He was at the fire station the day I was sterilised.
My parents later told me they could hear my cries from down the hallway,
"I'm barren. Now my husband really will leave me."

Later that night, I climbed the stairs- those same stairs where I had overheard those painful words- only to find I'd been locked out of our bedroom.
He was on the phone with another woman.

"We have to love each other enough not to destroy each other. You must leave."
'Really? You're kicking me out?'
"You already resent me. I don't want to resent you."

That surgery didn't take, and soon I was in ICU as he moved out.
I don't know that I've ever wailed like I did that first night I collapsed onto the threshold of my home after he left.
Once I got to my feet I walked the house, clutching my chest in fear of what I'd find.

Kindness.
I found kindness.
When I opened our closet door, he had spread out all of my clothes so that I wouldn't see holes where his had been.

This is a story very few know.
It's been...wow, a decade now, I suppose.
It's taken me this long to share it.
How long do you think it will take your coworkers to share theirs?

The coworker who stays late, who takes on more work- how do you know it's not so that they don't have to go home to an empty house bought for a different life?
How do you know that they aren't channeling all their energy, not to pose a threat to you, but because it's their lifeline?
How do you know if what looks like vanity, isn't actually sanity?

If, in all of that, he and I could find kindness, can't you?
It's not enough to read the room.
Or read another person.
You have to read yourself, too.
Actually, you have to do all three.
Simultaneously.

Ten

This morning was a very big Momma Mandolen Milestone. The #HoundAndTerrier needed to get boarded, only our regular boarder is on vacation which meant I needed to load up the baby, all the doggo things, and drive an hour round-trip to a new place.

My rescue Morkie, #GriffinTheTerrible, was on the floorboard of the front seat. While he's brave and wild here at the Haven, he shivers and pants whenever we go new places.
A holdover from the trauma he endured before he and I met.

Harbour was snuggled and playing with her mobile in the back seat. The trauma her nervous system was exposed to prior to meeting me seemingly not impacting her.

My #BadNewsBasset, Bilbo Baggins, was squinched into a crate in the back. The only one of us who has lived an absolutely charmed life and he was crying like a diva!

Me, thinking through all the things I'm forgetting.
The next steps to get ready and on the road for yet another trip to Mayo.
The papers I need to grade.
The clients I need to touch base with.
The emails…dear Lord, the emails.
Most people would be thinking "My life is a circus!"
I was thinking, 'Thank God we're all together.'

And then it struck me, as I sang along to George Ezra and kept repeating, "Good babies- such *GOOD* babies", that my little crew was taking cues from me.

"Momma, are we safe?" they seemed to be asking.
'Of course.' My voice and a touch on Griffin's fur seemed to answer.
I am responsible for crafting the environments they grow and thrive in.
I am their leader.

Earlier in my life my high energy was cause to amp up situations.
I was far too focused on reading others, or reading situations, to realise all the alarms going off in my body.
And, as my somatic experience therapist tells me, I soak up other people's emotions.
I wear them.
I drown in them.

For a long time, I didn't understand that.
I thought I was being empathetic without understanding that all those emotions I absorbed were then transferred into full-force energy, jumbled and intense.
If I just could show folks I cared enough, then I'd be able to help.
To make progress.
To do something!
BIG love.
BIG Grace.
BIG heart.

But I didn't know that in order to truly set the tone for others, I needed to calibrate myself first.
This morning, with everything else swirling around, I was calibrated, and, thus so were my babies.
These days I don't read the room or anyone else until I know what I'm bringing to the table at that moment.
It's been a massive lesson for me- and, apparently for others, a gift.

Eleven

For the first time, I had to cancel a talk last week- because I literally couldn't talk. Apparently having a newborn cough directly into your eyeballs is not good for the ol' immune system, folks.
(We're both fine, it's some kind of sinus drainage thing and I will say we're bonding in a big way over #MommyAndMighty ear massages.)

Now, rescheduling was well understood by the amazing group I was to talk with, Chronic Boss Collective. They get it, and they get me.
But, ya'll, here's the thing: I know how to work with my chronic illnesses (kinda) but I forget that I get the regular stuff, too.

Usually, I power through Crohn's flares.
I navigate around dystonia exacerbations.
I stay away from the sound of emergency sirens.
These things I'm working with- or working through- despite of.

I have tools, and while they don't always work effectively, they bring me confidence. After all, having my illnesses has taught me some things.
They taught me to get help.
To be kind to myself.
To trust my agility.
To know my limits.

But today I head back to Mayo again, for an unexpected appointment, in hopes that we can find an answer to the one thing I haven't been able to get tools for because no one knows why it's happening: Chronic hypoglycaemia.
For two years.
With no warning.
And seemingly no cause.

I'm fine. You and I are talking, laughing.
BAM!
Blood sugar crashes.
Glucose gels. Tablets. Candy. Juice. Nut butter pouches. Emergency injections/sprays. Cornstarch.
Sometimes these things work.
Sometimes they don't.

I've been to this specialist and that one.
I've undergone a 72-Hr hospital stay where I fasted and was stuck with needles every hour, on the hour, while we forced my blood sugar into critical levels.
Liver biopsy.
Mayo.
Genetic sequencing (in progress).
Everyone is puzzled.
I'm a research project.

For two years I've been dancing around, reactively treating something we haven't yet found out how to proactively avoid.
And I think about how I hate being reactive.
I hate "adapting".
These things feel like lazy work at best, and a total absconding of one's self-agency at worst.

I much prefer agility.
Proactive, not reactive.
Intentional, not instinctual.
Agile, not adaptive.
Like when I have confidence in myself and my tools to navigate obstacles.
As a Change Scientist, this is exactly what I train others to develop.

For two years, I've muddled through, avoiding critical outcomes despite critical blood sugar levels.
But my confidence in how much longer I can do that- in how useful my tools will be when I reach for them- isn't yet there.

Here's hoping I get it at Mayo.

Twelve

Patty Griffin was singing about a trapeze as I drove through the drizzle and bare-tree forest. Criss-crossing the river, I noticed it looked like a fogged up antique mirror reflecting my mood.
Dystonia gripping at my jaw and neck.
My chest feeling like an open wound.

Many of you knew this week would be difficult for me and you reached out.
You, surprisingly and kindly, sent gifts.
You comforted.

And comfort is important here as, after sitting alone all day while the baby I've loved with everything I am for 5 months drove away to meet her bio mother for the first time, I was bereft.

I called family.
No answer.
I called my over-protective Bestie.
She wanted to get out the knives.
I sobbed, "No, Rach, *NO!* Isn't there enough pain already? Haven't I experienced enough cruelty?"
This only prompted her to quote one of my favourite movies, 'Bring me the big knife.'

I told my therapist this week, "I realise everyone has challenges. Mine are no more or no less than others..."
To which they interrupted, 'It's more, Mandolen. You've endured more. I do this for a living and with all your family dynamics, your career twists, Crohn's, dystonia, car wreck, miscarriage, unexpectedly asked to adopt a baby and then told they were keeping it, divorce, feeding tubes, traumatic

surgeries, watching your father slowly die, and *NOW* unexpectedly asked to take this child with the expectation you'll adopt- by people who knew your history- only to be drug through this hell of her family trying to reunite her with the biological parent…it's more.'

That was a kindness I didn't know I needed.
Someone else to voice what I feel but if I say makes me sound whiney.
Ungrateful.
Less than 0.4% of Crohn's patients have the disease throughout their digestive system like I do.
Dystonia, 1% of the population gets it, and 1% of that 1% get acquired torsion, the form I have.
Less than 50% of people survive a rollover wreck.
The genetic disease Mayo is currently assessing me for has only 40 documented cases, making my odds 1 in 200 billion.
And yet, I work. I do great work, ya'll. I'm good because I care, genuinely.
And I'm a darn good mother, despite having less than 24 hours to prepare to be one.
The doggos have a ridiculously lavish life.
And I have amazing friends- when they keep the knives at bay.

But if my Obit was written today, it'd likely read, "She had a hard life."
And I think right now, I'm okay with voicing that.
Because this week was brutal.
Brutal.
And I'll have more weeks of this.
Of a life I didn't ask for and a love I cannot help but give, because treating my daughter as if she is temporary in my life deprives her of the development she needs and deserves.
I'm not willing to sacrifice her growth for my heart.
But I may be temporary in her life.
And it guts me.

Yes, I lean on my faith.
Yes, I take it one day at a time.
Yes, I'm learning patience.

But sometimes I think He asks too much of a person.
And, I suppose, that's why He sends friends.
Thank ya'll for being here.

Thirteen

Eighteen years ago today I woke up knowing I was very ill. Although I had been experiencing extreme fatigue for several months prior, nothing had ever felt like this. Like I had just swallowed razor blades.
Unable to keep food down, I lost 40lbs in mere weeks while doctors ran tests.
My hair started falling out.
My skin turned grey.
A rare form of severe Crohn's disease throughout my entire digestive tract.

Eleven years ago today I woke up in ICU. An endometrial ablation had gone awry, causing my uterus to melt together, resulting in sepsis.
I was alone, my husband having moved out just prior.
My parents drove up for a half-hour visit.
My employees drove two hours after pulling a 16-hour shift to bring me flowers.

Five years ago today I got the call that my father had cancer.
Four years ago today we found out it had returned.

A year ago today I spent the day alone- ignoring all calls/texts/voicemails as I surrounded myself with the ghosts of expectations and past dreams.
I felt lost and like a failure.
I insisted no one tell me it was a "happy" day as I didn't want sanguinity to intrude on my sour solitude.

And, 23 years ago today I received such an atrocious, pastel embroidered, denim vest that my best friend later read to our entire honours English class a poem she'd penned about its depravity.

I do not enjoy my birthday for these reasons.
And yet...lately I've been thinking on something, ya'll- particularly as I actively go through this week on the yo-yo of being an unexpected foster mother.

I've been called an inspiration by others.
Normally I bristle at that- because it is indeed the very trials of my Crohn's, dystonia, miscarriage, near-death experience, heart-wrenching motherhood journey, etc. that prompts people to think me as such.
And I think on that whole "He gives His greatest challenges to His strongest soldiers."
I've bristled at that, too.

But now I think maybe I've been misguided.
Maybe we become His strongest soldiers through those challenges.
Maybe being an inspiration means you endured.
You navigated.
You grieved in the silence of those seemingly endless dark nights.
You gave yourself Grace.
You kept going.
And somehow, miraculously, you became a better person, not a bitter one.

My trials are as serious and mundane as those marked by this day- same as anyone else's on any other days.
And yet, we have the distinct capacity to grow through all of that.
Not in some PollyAnna, toxically positive, disingenuous way- but in the way that says, "This sucks. And I'm allowed to feel distraught and discomforted by its suckiness. Yet I also know it won't suck forever. So, until it doesn't, I'll honour what I feel right now. Until those feelings pass on through."

I don't think there is Growth without Grace.
I don't think there is Hope without Hardship.

So, my birthday wish is this: May you find Grace, Growth, and Hope through whatever hardships come along.
I am cheering you on.

Fourteen

Self-care is lame.
Okay, maybe I'm being brash. But actually, the way in which we use that term is lame.
It's a buzzword, and I don't know if it means the same to you as it means to me.

I was driving through freshly churned cornfields yesterday while Van Morrison sang about comfort and all I could think about is the lessons I've been teaching to folks lately.
About how "self-care" and "stress-mitigation" feel like the wrong strategies.
About how I think that old Irishman is right.
"Comfort" seems more apt.

Look, I'm just like every other Millennial with my weighted blanket, lavender aromatherapy, and weekly therapy sessions. And for years I checked all the boxes of what all the gurus told me I was supposed to do in the almighty name of "self-care".
Only it didn't resonate.
It didn't work.
I went for walks.
I did Spa Days.
I curled up with a book with my little doggo creeps.
And I still didn't feel it.
Rested? Sure.
Recharged? Nope.

And it wasn't until about two years ago where, on some random "self-care" list, about halfway down the page, I saw it: *Take a hot shower and climb into clean bedsheets.*

Ya'll!
That. Was. It!
That *DOES* make me feel better after a bad day.
That does make me feel safe.
That does make me feel comforted.

And, so, having that feeling at the forefront, I then began to find other ways to replicate it.
Arranging cut flowers.
Wandering around my woods in prayer.
Sitting near water.
Hearing the sounds of live baseball.
Reading books to Harbour.
All of those things are like touchstones back to me. No matter what is going on in my life or the world, if I do those things, I'm recharging.
Refilling.

You know, I've realised I'd never seen adults seek out comfort after a stressful day.
Distraction? Disassociation? Disconnection?
Absolutely.
But not an actual way to refill what had been taken out of them.
Not a way to heal.

So, for me, it's not about "care", it's about "comfort".
Safety.
Belonging.
How we regulate ourselves, not with maladaptive behaviours that we've seen mimicked from others in our lives- the drinks, the doom-scrolling, the online shopping.
But the truly regenerative and restorative actions that fills us up with all the good feelings.

I think until we can get on the same page of understanding what "self-care" actually is for each individual, we don't move the needle.
And that's a shame.
Because everyone deserves to feel comforted.
Van said so.
And one should always listen to the Irish.

Fifteen

He told me he had three stacks: Those for sure that were being admitted, those for sure not to be admitted, and then the middle stack was for the folks in between.

That last one contained my application.

"Do you know what it takes to be successful in a doctoral program?"

'No sir, I do not. I've never been in one before. But, I suspect it requires *StickWithItness* and *GRIT*, which stands for Girl Raised in Texas. Sir, I have severe Crohn's disease and have built a career and earned an MBA with it. I don't know what a Ph.D. is going to require of me, but if you're looking for commitment, I'm committed. Don't count me out.'

I, along with 8 others, got accepted that year.

I had no idea during that phone call 9 years ago that the following year I'd be diagnosed with acquired torsion dystonia. Unable to control my muscles, I had someone drive me the 8-hour round-trip to sit through 16 hours of doctoral coursework every three weeks.

Walking with a cane, struggling to speak, fighting the brain fog of anti-seizure medications, I earned a 4.0.

Outstanding Student of the Year.

I consulted.

I presented and published research.

I continued to work, carrying a heavy workload (two people were hired to fill my role when I later resigned to assume a faculty position).

I graduated just over 3 years from that phone call.

Don't. Count. Me. Out.

But that's not the story.

The story is the 8 others.

And how, the night before our first class session I had suggested a dinner for us to meet each other.
I pulled up to the restaurant in my decade-old Xterra and parked beside Range Rovers and Mercedes.
As I met everyone, I realised I was the youngest in the cohort.
I was also the only one without any background in our field.
Right as our meal was being served, I remarked, "Ya'll- I'm terrified about all of this."
The man next to me lowered his head and said, 'Thank God someone said it-I am too!'

What ensued was a conversation about insecurities, vulnerabilities, and eventually, a commitment to each other: We were going to do this together. We'd identify those who were better at stats, writing, interviewing, and they'd tutor the rest.
We chose a hotel where we spent each class weekend, staying up late at night to review each other's work for the next day and waking up early to share breakfast together.

All of us graduated in the same year.

We later found out that we were all "in the middle stack".
Apparently it was some old sales trick by our Director to see how much we wanted the opportunity.
But you know, I don't think he needed that to prove our commitment.
I think he just needed to put us in a room and let us be vulnerable.

Sixteen

Fat snowflakes crushed against the windshield as I wound through the forest of white pines. Gusts of wind buffeted my car while Tyler Childers sang about a Long Violent History.

It was crappy weather. Weather that had flickered the Haven's power and knocked out the Internet.

I should've been frazzled.

But it's not the bad, dreary, days that get me.

It's the sunny, normal, ones.

Three years ago I traded in my car. I'll be honest, I wasn't entirely discerning on the type.

I just wanted something safe.

Three weeks later, less than 24 hours after a 5-day hospital stint- I was careening around a racetrack at over a hundred miles per hour. I'd come to support one of my students, a professional driver.

Wearing a helmet in the passenger seat as I tried to be cool, he showed me his craft.

Upon snapping a photo with his family, I headed home.

And then my world turned upside down.

Once.

Twice.

Again.

Again.

An eyewitness said they saw the bottom of my car 4 times and prepared for the worst.

A neighbour said, upon hearing the multiple impacts my vehicle made on the earth, "I thought, 'My God- they are hitting her over and over!'"

From inside, as glass fell around me, and my seatbelt gripped tight, I saw the driver who ran the stop sign standing in the road watching.
They were safe.
When I realised the roof was caving in, I put my hands up as I yelled out to God, "Please don't do this to my parents!"

Sirens came.
I was cut out of the car.
I was cut out of my clothes.
The tow truck driver and crash inspector couldn't believe I was alive.

Tire marks burned into the asphalt of where I tried to avoid the collision.
My mangled car shown on the evening news.

I had Mayo in 2 weeks.
I had class to teach the next day.
Daddy was dying.

I was told I was lucky.
I had to keep going.

But then sirens came.
They still come.
Like another assault.
The PTSD brings back jagged, glass-like, memories and images, electrifying my nervous system like a Christmas tree, exacerbating my dystonia as muscles painfully contort.
The confusion and disorientation of how I could be doing everything right, and something go so terribly wrong…

I'm grateful I survived. But it wasn't without pain I continue to work through.

Because it's not the tough days that get me.
It's the normal ones.
The ones where I think I am in control.
Until the unexpected brings twists and turns.

I think a lot of folks live with paradoxes like that. Because we were taught linearly.
If I do A, B will occur.
If I'm a good person, good things happen. (The converse for us Southerners with Catholic guilt is that if something bad happens, well, we must be bad.)

It's not often the days and ways in which we expect things to go wrong that do.
It's the ones we never see coming.

I think one of the hardest things for us to do is to Unlearn. To reduce our reliance on past experiences as predictors of future outcomes.
Unlearn our beliefs.
Our reactions.
Our neural pathways.
Our expectations.

Seventeen

It's a strange thing to feel like you don't belong in a room- but also that you absolutely do. I had the honour of speaking at #WomenInRare.
I was asked to speak on Imposter Syndrome as MullMentum.
Only Mandolen, the patient waiting for genetic sequencing to confirm that the last 18 years of her life has been the result of a smooth muscle disease in which there's only 40 cases documented, had never been in a room like that.

A room of women changing the world as they advocate for their children, for other people's children, for themselves, for others like themselves.
Women who've crafted legislation, championed drug trials, written books, given TedTalks.
The most incredible women, ya'll.

Despite both a Crohn's and dystonia flare, I spoke.

Nervous energy flew all around me as I jumbled my presentation. I leaned into the fact that I felt like an Imposter- both as someone measuring myself to their amazing hearts and talents, and as someone who is sick, but not (in my mind) sick enough. I listened to their remarkable stories and I kept getting in my own way as I wanted to cry and hug them and thank them and give them all my support and energy and...all the things.

Stuck in that head and heart space, I made the mistake of looking at my phone.
An email notifying me I must change my plans as Harbour is to see her bio mom.
And my muscles began to twist.
The ulcers in my stomach coiled.

Six months ago I was asked to take care of a baby, after miscarrying and traumatic surgeries. Not on a foster list, I had less than 24 hours of notice.
For months I've given my little girl everything I have.
While running a company.
While navigating my health.

But I'm in a situation that keeps me suspended in being an impermanent mother, unconcerned about the grief it brings.
A situation that asked me to "jump" and I did.
Then asks me jump some more.
I'm to give 100% to my baby who deserves that, while a situation that disregards my life actively disrupts it.

It is cruel.
Cruel to spend 18 years in a medical system that has gaslit and misdiagnosed me.
Cruel that I've fought through, and forward, only to be brought to my knees.
Cruel to dangle hope in front of me, only to drag me along in uncertainty.
And it's cruel to Harbour, who deserves this amazing mother who cobbles together massive, loving, energy despite health issues, work, and being an overnight unexpected solo mother- but is a temporary, disposable, placeholder.
Whose heart keeps telling her otherwise.
But it doesn't get a say.

I'm a business on the stage.
A woman crying in the bathroom.
A child asking, "Why have you called me to serve in so many realms? Where it takes everything I have to show up in each before I shift to the next? Where the only thing I feel good at, you may take away?"

My story is different than the women I spoke to...but in many ways, it's not.
And somehow they've found the strength to keep going.
So, I guess, somehow, I will, too.

Summer 2024

One

Because she had makeup on and was dressed nicely, her child- who battles a rare genetic disease- was denied federal assistance.
For four years.

This issue is similar to something my former husband used to fuss at me about, "I see you curled up in a ball on the couch, rushing to the bathroom, not eating. Everyone else sees you dressed to the nines. And, after you've gone out into the world and shone your light, you have none left to shine when you get home."

It's a constant battle.
Has been for 18 years now on this chronic health journey.
I have to dress nice enough so that people will take me seriously.
But if I dress too nicely, then I must not really be sick.
I have to be pleasant so that folks will want to help me.
But if I'm too pleasant, then it's easy to push me aside.
Squeaky wheels and all that.
And I have to work to pay all that medical debt incurred when my adult life was just beginning.
And the student loan debt taken on in a hope of remaining a contributing member of society with a more flexible schedule accommodating my illnesses (back then, remote work wasn't really an option for folks like me- a population disproportionately disadvantaged in RTO environments as we often need reasonable medical accommodations that employers aren't willing to offer).

But if I work too hard, I get more sick.
I've got to go out on stage and inspire- trying to turn my stumbling blocks into stepping stones.

But the peanut gallery watches from afar and says, "See! She can give a one-hour keynote so she's clearly faking being sick."

The amount of gaslighting and discrimination I've faced because my disabilities aren't always visible...ya'll!
It's as if multiple things cannot be true at once.
And I'm not alone.
Not by a long shot.

Two

I suppose in comparison, it actually isn't a poor way of coping with things.
I thought about that as Gregg Allman sang about soulshine being better than moonshine as I drove alongside the flooded river.
New life springing out all around me, so verdant it almost hurts the eyes.

I was recently told that, in light of my current circumstances, "all of (my) traditional coping skills aren't options".
Restriction.
Retreat.

As an unexpected overnight foster mother, I live in uncertainty of if the only daughter I've ever had- will ever have- will always be mine.
As an entrepreneur I live with the uncertainty of if another client will come along, or one no longer remains.

As Mayo continues the 2-3 month genomic sequencing on my DNA, I live with the uncertainty that at any moment a call or MyChart message may come and disrupt my life.

In prior experiences of such impactful uncertainty I could retreat into my work.
I could restrict access to those in my life.
I could, I suppose, find control when the uncontrollable emerged.

As a child, I never knew when my Daddy- and later my sister, who inherited his temper- would go off.
Or when my mother would close up.
So my books and my study were my escape.

When I miscarried and my husband left, I retreated to my work.

When I could no longer digest solid foods, I restricted what I ate.

When my Daddy's cancer returned, I drove up to a secluded lake-front cabin and spent two weeks alone without wifi...as soon as I drove away and my cell connected, I learned the world was shutting down due to Covid.

And, last October when I felt restless in regards to my purpose in life, I set off on a 7-state #WanderingRoadTrip.

When I returned, I became a mother.

My sanctuary, my Haven in the Woods, brings its own uncertainty.

Mischievous doggos who answer to no one.

A rapidly growing bebe who keeps me on my toes as I keep trying to anticipate and predict her future needs (I asked my mother how she knew to lower our crib "Whenever you stood up", she replied. I informed her that seemed a terribly reactive indicator for safety!).

Old trees that uproot and block the drive.

And I cannot restrict or retreat.

But, you know, I do think Gregg was on to something.

Most folks don't know what their coping skills are- let alone know how to tap into healthy ones.

But I think the most important thing to know is, sometimes there's nothing to "fix" or alleviate.

Sometimes we just gotta sit with it.

And let our soul shine.

Three

Shards of orange poked through bare branches as I drove alongside the bloated river, the emerging sun turning it silver and bronze. In the backseat I could see Harbour dancing along to Cody Jinks as he sang about being somewhere in the middle.

In a month my father will have been gone for two years.
These milestones are so strange.
You don't really think about them and then suddenly you remember...

In many ways it feels like my father just left. Like we had one of our coffee chats this past weekend.
In others, it feels like he's been gone an entire lifetime.
Or, at least the lifetime of the granddaughter he never got to meet.

My Daddy had this quirky way of starting a conversation like you were in the middle of one. There'd be silence as he worked on blueprints and I read a book. Then, all of the sudden, "And that's another thing, baby, that idiot down at the lumber yard! Man, I tell ya..."
While I'd be busy thinking 'Was there a first thing?! Who is the idiot? What did I miss?' he'd just keep right on with the rest of the story.

No preamble.
Just dropped you right into the middle.
And kept moving forward.

His death was like that.
Cancer came without any symptoms. And while we knew for three years it was going to take him, he kept beating it back.
He kept bouncing back.

In fact, when I was called home for the final goodbye, I arrived to find him eating a chicken fried steak dinner.
I thought there had to be some mistake.
Surely a dying man wouldn't be eating waffle fries.
The juxtaposition was inexplicably jarring.

I'm realising a lot of things in my life have been that way: dropped into the middle of an ongoing scene.
Crohn's.
Dystonia.
Car wreck.
Motherhood.
One day I was just me, and then...
I was sick for the rest of my life.
I was told I'd be unable to walk, talk, or feed myself within 5 years (in October, that will have been 8 years ago!).
My world was upside down and all sense of safety shattered like the glass that fell on me.
I was going to be a mom.
Then I wasn't.
Then I never would be.
Then I became one overnight.
One day I may not be, once again.

And maybe the lack of the preamble is a blessing- we don't get enough time to really understand what is happening.
Or, maybe the lack of the preamble is a curse- we don't get enough time to really understand what is happening.
But either way, despite the jarring nature of it all, despite the seemingly disjointed disconnection, it seems rather...*human*.

I don't know, ya'll, but I'm starting to think some of our deepest moments are in the duality.
That space where we hold competing and incongruent emotions.
I think that's where we grow the most.
In the middle.

Four

I have a doctorate in change, which is ironic considering that for the majority of my life I was pretty resistant to it. Oh, and also, I had to learn to walk and talk again while getting my doctorate, meaning I had a whole bunch of change to navigate while learning about change.
That kind of fits the comedy of my life, doncha think?

You see, it was the fall of my second year when I started noticing I was skipping words, bumping into walls, dragging my leg, and having muscle spasms that lasted for hours.
One day my toes flattened and inverted.
Another, my left arm curled up.
I figured I was just tired.
But one morning I went to work and when a colleague spoke to me, I replied...only I didn't.
My words were garbled.
My jaw hurt and my tongue, frozen in an arch.

Eventually, I was diagnosed with acquired torsion dystonia.
I was given 5 years before I would be severely deformed by the muscle contractions.
I was told bones may fracture.
Teeth would need to be extracted.
That there was no standard treatment and if I were to have any hope, I had to make progress that first year.

In many ways, I think I was able to get to where I am today because a decade prior to dystonia I woke up one morning and knew something was seriously wrong.
Months later I was diagnosed with severe Crohn's.

For the first time in my life, I realised there was no "going back to before".

And today I'm not severely deformed by my dystonia...but I'm also not pre-dystonia Mandolen.
I take multiple medications.
I get Botox injected throughout my body.
I do physical therapy.
It helps, but dystonia still disrupts my life at random.
Just like Crohn's.

These were changes in my life I didn't ask for.
Yet, I couldn't resist them.
I had to learn how to grow forward, altered by these uninvited guests.
I had to learn who I was with their accompaniment in my life.
It wasn't always pretty.
Sometimes it still isn't.

Folks hear me say "Even positive change is disruptive".
It is.

Folks hear me say "The world will never be short of shitheads and shitshows because there's always another ready to take its place. So you cannot allow yourself to be discombobulated and distracted each time one comes around."
Very true.

Yet what I'm trying to say in my health narrative and my quippy quotes is that: Change is.
It is.
So expect it.
Embrace it.
Go with it.
Grow with it.

Five

There's a squirrel roaming my woods that has half a tail. I've thought about the reasons for this more than I should, ya'll.
And I am reminded of a call I had years ago with my dear friend Robin.

"Hun, what's wrong?"
'Well, it's just that the two turkeys that walk the yard every morning? There's only one today...'
"M, we've talked about this. What did I tell you?"
'Don't get attached to the wildlife at the Haven.'
"Don't get attached to the wildlife at the Haven!" Robin repeated for good measure.

But of course I do.
And this particular squirrel...what exactly IS his story?
Was he born that way?
Was there some death-defying predator encounter?
Was there a hilarious yet painful snag?

Does he have some kind of health problem and should I try to capture him and take him to an animal rescue? (I'm not going to do this, ya'll, but it has absolutely crossed my mind.)

I don't know.
And I think about this silly squirrel and how he's teaching me things I don't know about the folks I encounter.
Were they born that way?
Are they victors of some trauma?
Have they developed through adversity?

Do they have some exigent need to be addressed and yours truly should swoop in and save them? (I'm not going to do this, ya'll, but it has absolutely crossed my mind.)

Each morning I watch him and he seems happy, if not a little addle-minded in his foraging for food...although, I cannot entirely say all squirrels don't appear that way.
He doesn't seem aware that half his tail isn't there.
It doesn't seem to inhibit him or slow him down.
And so, while it doesn't affect him- it does affect me.

But then that has me wondering how often we are affected by things that happen to others, yet they themselves are unaffected by.
Much like my considerations of trying to insert myself into situations where my gifts are not required.
Those considerations, which actually are quite inconsiderate.

Early in my Crohn's and Dystonia diagnoses I had well-meaning loved ones tell me not to speak about my illnesses.
"People will think less of you. They'll think you can't be productive or dependable. They'll think you're a liability."
These folks meant well.
And, so, I learned to respond, 'Trust me enough to tell you when I'm in over my skis. Believe in me enough that I can do anything I say I can do. Support me enough that others trust and believe in me because you do.'

Being curious about this squirrel's missing tail is fine.
Trying to save him, when he hasn't asked me to and seems entirely uninterested in me doing so, isn't.
Everyone deserves to be supported...but not everyone wants to be.
And that's probably one of the hardest lessons I've ever learned.

Six

In my defense, there weren't any instructions. Actually, that's kind of a crappy defense considering that I don't read instructions...unless I'm cooking.
Which in itself is such a rare event that I get nineteen kinds of ignorant whenever I do.

"Why didn't you just Google how to make them?" my friend Anna asked from my phone on the kitchen island where it was laying next to the charred mess of my attempted dinner.
'Anna, my only discernible skill in life is being smart.' I replied.
I changed accents as I began to imitate my Daddy, "I have two daughters, one very book smart but not common sense smart!"
(For the record, my elder sister Darby was, according to him, neither. Her scrappy nature was deemed "street smart").

I rubbed my hand across my face.
An idea sparked!
'I mean...they are called Black Pearl crab...?'
"Mandolen, no! *Stop!* You cannot be serious right now! I literally thought, 'Surely she doesn't think they are supposed to be black because of the name. Surely!' Oh Mandolen...no."

Again, my only discernible skill is being smart, ya'll.
Only, "smart" is just relegated to random theories and analogies.
Book smart.
And I definitely always opt for working harder, not smarter, which is why my dinner went up in flames.
Because I just like to jump in.
Figure it out.
Learn as I go.

Which is why I always feel a little intimidated and insecure when other consultants ask me what models I use.

"I don't."

What assessments I use.

"I don't."

So...what do I do?

"I just go talk to folks. I ask their pain points and go from there. I've built up enough applied knowledge over the years that I trust I'll be able to offer something insightful. Something useful and resonating. Something current and tangible."

Those that know me best know I cannot drive anywhere- **ANYWHERE**- without my GPS talking to me along the way (the only instructions I follow, but only in real-time as I never look ahead).

They know I will confidently tackle any house project with gusto and without any clue whatsoever of what I'm actually doing which always takes me twice as long as I figure out what directions would've saved me time on.

They know I'm prone to traipsing off into my woods with shears and a water bucket to collect flowers, completely oblivious to ticks or the myriad poisonous leaves/shrubs that dot my woods.

And they know I burn my food on my annual attempt.

I don't read instructions.

I don't use models or strategies.

I definitely make things harder than they have to be.

But you know, I like these quips and quirks.

I think many of us follow the guidelines, colour within the lines, entrench ourselves, a bit too much.

I think we follow the expectations and paths laid out for us.

I think we get too locked into directions and don't do enough creative work. We don't trust ourselves enough to figure things out as they come.

Look ya'll, I'm not saying burn your dinner, but I am saying it's a small price to pay for doing things your way.

Seven

Griffin keeps dead-legging me.
Actually, it's not just me.
He crashes into walls, into his basset hound brother Bilbo Baggins, into my shrubbery.

You see, my little rescue Morkie had a trip to the groomer's last week and now his fluffy, curled-over-his-back, tail seems to be a wee bit difficult for him to navigate.
He's top-heavy.
He's off kilter.
He's making a mess just trying to do an everyday thing he's handled previously without issue.

I'm reminded of how we shouldn't touch butterflies because in doing so, we remove some of their brilliant colouring, rendering them unable to fly correctly.

So of course, this makes me think of people and the stress they carry.
Unlike my little man Grif, or beautiful monarchs, it's not usually one particular cause that weighs folks down.
It's usually accumulated stress.
Allostatic load.

If we think about incremental change, such as that most recently popularised by Clear's "Atomic Habits", we can flip that and consider how incremental stress alters a person in much the same way, only to a negative degree.

I know in my life I've often said, "But I don't *FEEL* stressed! I've been through heavier things before."

And I have been told, 'Exactly. You've been through them, but you didn't let them go. Their residue remains. And of course you don't feel stressed- your body has been conditioned to not know any other operating mode.'

So how do we combat it?
We find our personal brand of self-care to act as a pressure release.
A place where we offload the weight and peel off the residue.

Grif does that by finding safety in solid things to hold him up.
I do it by taking a hot shower and crawling into clean bed sheets with a book.
I do it by waking my doggos through the woods, looking for wildlife and flowers while singing to the boys as if I'm some character from a Disney movie (if anyone ever stumbles upon me, my face will be redder than my hair!).
I do it by dramatically acting out stories to Harbour, while she watches wide-eyed and giggling as if I'm the greatest toy she's ever discovered.
I do it by going to therapy to learn coping skills I never saw modelled for me.
I do it by leaning into my faith.
I do it by writing.

Whatever it is that is **YOUR** brand of safety and self-care, I hope it brings you great comfort and strength.
I'm cheering you on.

Eight

Tom Petty sang about the hardest part as I watched chipmunks play peek-a-boo in the tree outside my kitchen. "I. Was. Made. For. This." kept shouting through my thoughts; equalling the shouts of pain from my stress-induced dystonic muscle cramps.

I was made for this.

Several years ago a close friend of mine had told me about their child who was being bullied at school. I offered my support and willingness to share my insights and encouragement.
The response I got was incredible: "Mandolen, I appreciate that. And I'll reach out if I think I need backup. But, I was bullied- so much so that I still carry physical effects. I endured all of that to be able to say today, 'No one gets to make my child feel less than.' I. Was. Made. For. This."

Over the years I have often wondered at the challenges I have endured. My southern Baptist upbringing having me searching for whatever sins I committed to deserve the punishment.
At least that would make sense of the insensible...

This strategy even played out as my Daddy battled cancer. A yo-yo battle where he beat it only for it, or the effects of the treatment, to take him to death's door and back.
For three agonising years.
"God is punishing me for what I did to ya'll. I deserve this- but ya'll don't." he told my mother.
"God does not work that way." she told him back.

Crohn's.
Miscarriage.
Surgeries.
Divorce.
Dystonia.
Feeding tubes.
Continued malnutrition.
Distracted driver.
Emergency sirens that, to this day, light up my nervous system.
Hope of motherhood dangled and lost- again and again.
There's a battle that I navigate today: I endured all of that because I was made for this.
God punishes.
God doesn't work that way.

The waiting, truly, is the hardest part.

And I post about these things because I think this is human.
I think many- if not all- of us wrestle with these combatants.
I think many-if not all- of us sit in the waiting and try to turn it into a positive.
Into something faithful and faith filled.

Overall, the loudest voice I keep hearing- keep feeling- is: I. Was. Made. For. This.
So were you.

Nine

It's the posts I don't want to write, the most vulnerable ones, where someone sends a DM of "I needed to read that".
And this one?
I really don't want to write.

In the fall of 2019 I was holding in immense stress.
A rookie thrown into the chaos of academic administration, my father's cancer returning, navigating a failed relationship, and I couldn't eat.
Every time I tried, my stomach would painfully swell making me look pregnant.
Eventually, I told myself, "You know better and have too much going on to deal with this. Just stop eating."
So I did.

As my weight dropped, I began to obsess over numbers.
How many calories.
How many miles.
How low the dress size.
My friends hid my scale as I dreamed about food- my body trying to get my attention.
I didn't know this was a survival instinct.

My doctors ruled out my Crohn's.
They ruled out my gastroparesis.
They ruled out bacteria.
And, years later, someone realised it was a paralysed diaphragm.
Possibly from my dystonia.
Possibly from scar tissue.
Possibly from what Mayo now investigates.

They realised that...but not after they diagnosed me with an eating disorder. An eating disorder caused by the untreated paralysed diaphragm.

By the time I got to the folks who could help, I was in bad shape.
Muscle loss.
Hair and nails falling off.
Sluggish brain.
Heart rate slow.
Blood pressure low.
I was told I needed to be admitted to the hospital as nutrition was restored. But the only place in the US that does that denied me because my BMI was fine for my height.
An adult being assessed as the same size of a 9-year old...

So I was told I needed to go to an Eating Disorder centre. A place where, if I didn't eat, I'd have a tube shoved up my nose and force fed.
A place where my physical health conditions would be ignored and me claimed as just being obstinate.
"Do you really think this is right?" I asked my doctor who had told me she couldn't believe I was surviving, let alone still thriving in my work.
She replied, 'You don't fit the diagnosis-but you're in dangerous territory.'
I asked for her help.
She committed.
I went and bought ice cream.
And we beat it back.

The amount of medical gaslighting I've experienced is...incalculable.
The doctors who have believed in me...incredible.
When a doctor told me this week, 'I'm overwhelmed listening to all you endure. I cannot imagine what it is like to live it," it wasn't the first time one had said that.

There were so many times I could've fallen through the cracks, ya'll: GI issues, dystonia, trauma, cancer, autonomic dysfunction, unexplained...so many unexplained symptoms.
We wait for Mayo's genomic test results...

And I don't know if I'm just stubborn or blessed.
I don't know if there's a purpose to it all or if I just have Irish bad luck.
But I know it matters in how you look at it.
I know it matters when you have folks who believe in you.
When you believe in you.

So if it's you- I believe.
But believe in yourself more.
Keep going forward.
And keep growing forward.

Ten

If Paul Harvey taught us anything, it's that there is most assuredly "the rest of the story."

In the summer of 2016 I began to notice the hand tremors.

By fall, folks saw me bumping into walls and dragging my leg behind me.

Then the spasms began.

And I lost the ability to speak correctly.

Eventually, I was told I'd be severely disabled within 5 years.

A few months ago, almost 8 years later, I had the opportunity to share that story on the #OnOneCondition podcast.

But, indeed, that was not the rest of the story...

"You sound more British today-what's been going on?" my doctor asked as he evaluated me. Because...in recent months, I've endured more.

More spasms.

More skipped words.

My toes flattening and inverting.

Charlie horses that last for hours.

Sometimes days.

My speech frustratingly fluctuating.

My doctors gave me new meds.

More Botox injections.

More therapy sessions in case all the stress of navigating a foster situation I never expected to be in was an exacerbating factor.

An MRI was ordered.

A spinal tap is next.

I'm assured by my medical team that right now nothing is urgent.

That I can keep taking care of myself and, most importantly, Harbour (and the doggos).

We await any day now the genomic sequencing results from Mayo where the geneticist was especially interested in my past MRI findings.

Where it's suspected I have a rare disease of which there have only been 40 documented cases.

Where, with a sample size that small, we're building the plane while it's flying.

I'd like to tell you this hasn't scared me.
That I didn't have reservations about posting this latest update.
That my "success" story of beating the odds doesn't now feel a bit farcical.
I'd like to tell you that.
But I can't.
Because it wouldn't be the truth.

And the truth is I have no idea what is next.
Nor do my doctors.
But...none of us really know these things, right?

I have been through the medical grinder for 18 years. Many touch-and-gos. Many lonely nights in hospitals with nothing but my fear and faith to keep me company.
And I was resourceful.
And resilient.
And I didn't have the support network then that I have today.
I didn't have the awareness then that I have today.
I didn't have the knitted tapestry of brilliant, empathetic, and wily rogue doctors then that I have today.

So despite all I lacked then, I got through those valleys to here because I had a purpose.

All those other setbacks were leveraged by a drive of mentorship.
Of work.
My purpose today?
Still the same actually: To develop leaders who go on to develop other leaders.
Of mentorship.
Only I call it something different now...Motherhood.

So, onward I go to discover the rest of the story.
We'll find it out together.

Eleven

They didn't understand in the beginning that I was sick. And, later, when they fully knew, the guilt was an albatross they carried.

In hindsight my parents would recount where they "missed" the signs.
They hung their head as they recalled the times they deemed me melodramatic or a hypochondriac.
The time they had me lay down while they pressed on my abdomen as I screamed and pulled their fingers away.
The time the school nurse called to take me to a doctor who wrote off my symptoms as "probably female issues", resulting in them getting upset with me for wasting everyone's time.
Many, many, years later, the late night calls came.
"I'm so sorry. We just didn't know."

There were surgeries.
The miscarriage.
Hospital stays.
Infusions and injections.
More diagnoses.
By the time dystonia came and I was unable to walk or talk, phone calls weren't returned.
It was "too hard" to hear my voice.
"Too hard" to see me with my sparkly cane.

I was angry.
And alone.
I thought I was a disappointment.
I didn't realise they were disappointed in themselves.

It's amazing what we achieve when we communicate the things we carry.
There were blowups.
Harsh words.
And, at some point, understanding- on both sides.

Daddy's cancer opened much of the door as I helped Momma navigate insurance.
And when we thought we beat it, my strong as an ox father held his stomach as he said, "Baby, you deal with this every day. You're my **HERO**, Wink."
I tried to tell him it wasn't comparable.
He brushed it aside, his mind made up.
Literally any day now I'm going to get a notification with the results of my genome sequencing.
If Daddy was alive, I've no doubt he would've personally delivered his mouth swab.
My Momma was so nervous that she consulted with others to ensure her DNA was accurately submitted.
My sister, not worried about what the results may mean for her and her boys, tells me how she wishes she could do more.
They now know what I kept from them for years: This path is scary, painful, and lonely.
Today, they stand in the arena with me.

We didn't get it "right" in real time, ya'll.
Mired in misunderstandings, misinterpretations, messiness.
I still sometimes see their guilt, and I try to meet it with Grace.
Because I need it, too.

At some point I learned to quit asking for help.
To quit sharing the specifics.
To stop saying I was scared.
And that only led to them not being able to help.

There's this quote from General Powell, "The day the soldiers stop bringing you their problems is the day you stopped leading them. They have either lost confidence that you can help them or concluded that you do not care. Either case is a failure of leadership."

My family didn't fail me.
They didn't know what to do.
And, I, like them, "...just didn't know."

There may be those folks in your life.
Maybe you, too, are like I was- keeping them out because you think they can't help.
Or worse, they don't care to.
And maybe-just maybe- there's more that ya'll "just don't know".

Twelve

My muscles unraveled as the woodwinds and horns played the notes of the iconic intro. My familiar friends Leo and Josh spoke quickly as the camera followed them through the West Wing.
It's interesting how these characters -much like those of my beloved Mitch Albom books- always seem like waiting friends, ready to pick up where we left off, whenever I stop by to visit them again.

That's a personal feeling, you know?
That familiarity.
And, I suppose, that's why so many find familiar things within these Mullings.
"You should write about that- about how folks thought today's post was about their workplace," my friend Sue told me last night.

And I wasn't going to write about that.
Today I was going to write about how Catcher, the son I carried but who wasn't born, would've been 15 this past Tuesday.
How today marks the 3rd year milestone of my horrific encounter with a distracted driver.
How we carry ourselves through trials and challenges yet we also carry those trials and challenges with us.
And that, too, is personal.
Familiar.

For about a year now I've been writing these Mullings each day.
Random mind anchors that crop up in reflection.
The timeline all scattered.
The themes, random.

The only commonality between topics is the fact that they are about my life and observations, which means somehow they always tie back into leadership.
They, like me, are rambling and unstructured.

But folks seem to resonate with my stream-of-consciousness.
And some take umbrage.
Once, I was accused of writing about something in my life as part of my "business model".
Like I even HAVE a business model, ya'll!
And yesterday's post about a leader weaponising their influence yielded three separate messages- from totally different aspects of my life- asking if my post was about someone they knew or their own workplace.
It wasn't.
Yet I think it speaks a lot to the prevalence of what we're seeing in our world.
What we're all collectively experiencing.

I think folks see the personal in my Mullings and maybe that's why it feels personal to them.
But if the shoe fits?
Well, it ain't because I'm a cobbler, ya'll.

I started writing these messages as a way to hold myself accountable.
To hold up a mirror to myself.
To ensure I was staying anchored to my values.
It seems that in the process of doing so, it's helped others be accountable as well.

I love the West Wing not only for its brilliance, but because those characters carried me through a lot.
Now I carry them as a touchstone.
They were the topic of many discussions with my grandparents.

They were real.
They connected us.
They connected with us.
They were familiar.
They still are.

I think if we look hard enough, we can find familiarity in any story.
I think we can find ourselves there, too.

So, friends, it isn't a cobbler making the shoe fit.
It is us looking in the mirror.
And then courageously doing something about it.

Thirteen

"Are you Mandolen?" I got asked by a stranger as I was checking out at the optometrist's office last week. My head down and bracing for an impact, I responded in a singsong voice that did not match my sudden cautiousness, "I am Mandolen."

Fortunately, the reason this stranger asked me about who I was is because she's the sister of one of my absolute favourite humans: My former consulting trainee who has become a forever friend, Bob.
So, clearly, I had no other option than to hug her.

See, but, these things always get me, ya'll.
Because despite having a well-known presence and good reputation, I rarely run into folks I know when I'm out and about locally these days.
That's a gift to this girl who grew up in a small southern town and couldn't go anywhere without seeing about a dozen people who either knew me or my family.
My large family of whom I was related to pretty much anyone who wasn't a transplant.
Heaven forbid I went out in gym clothes or without makeup- my mother notified before I even crossed the threshold at home.

But it wasn't just that this person last week seemed to know who I was, it's that since I've been posting my Mullings on here I've also been running into folks who say, "I read your stuff on LinkedIn."
Which, truth be told, almost immediately makes me cringe.
And despite the fact that statement is almost always followed by kind words, I still cringe every time.
Thank God ya'll don't have my Momma's phone number...

And here's the thing I've been Mulling on ever since that happened:
Certainly there's no anonymity in a forum like this.
And transparency and authenticity are two of my personal values, prompting me to write how and what I write here.
But despite showing up here the same way I do in person, my Imposter Syndrome- my insecurity- has me thinking, "If they knew me, they wouldn't like me."
Ah.
And what is it I think folks wouldn't like?
That I'm quirky.
A lot of nervous energy channeled into something people think is charming and charismatic but is genuinely me just trying not to be a whole bunch of awkward.
Someone who talks with her hands as much as she talks from her heart.

And here folks can keep scrolling.
Can anonymously unfollow.
But rejection in real life?
Ewww.

Kafka once wrote, "I was ashamed of myself when I realised that life was a costume party, and I attended with my real face."
That resonates so much with me, ya'll.
But you know, I'm not ashamed for attending with my real face.
I'm ashamed of how much weight I still give to others' in their perception- and acceptance- of me.

So this week, I'm digging deeper into that.
I hope you do, too.

Fourteen

The sun glinted off of diamonds of broken promises as Zach Bryan sang about Oklahoma City. The humidity rising from the river created a curtain within the forest I drove through.
Transforming my hair into the likeness of someone auditioning for the lead role of The Lion King.
"...I told her that you moved way out West to write some songs,
And grow a little more bitter."

I drove past a tree that had twisted into pieces.
Limbs and leaves scattered across the roadway.
I passed by the collapsed gas station awning where The Bestie and I had been just hours before.
The debris and destruction all part of the heavy winds that had blown in with the summer storm.

I began to search.
Surely I'd soon find a tree uprooted, just like the one in my woods from a winter storm last year.
But I couldn't find one.
I found many in various states of change, though.
Broken.
Tangled.
Dangling.
Blemished, really, more than battered.
Damaged, rather than destroyed.

Six years ago this week, nearing the end of my Ph.D., I packed up my three basset hounds (Boomer, Doc Holliday, Bilbo Baggins) and pulled out of the cul-de-sac of my beautiful Austin home.

Eighteen hours later I arrived in the MidWest to a property I hadn't even seen pictures of.
It wasn't the first time I uprooted.

As a child I escaped into my books.
To my grandparents.
To my closet corner.
And, at 18, I left.

When he came home a month before our one year anniversary and said it was too hard being married to a sick woman, I couldn't uproot or escape.
So I closed up.
When the next week we found out we were pregnant and he stayed, I waited for the other shoe to drop.
Months later, no heartbeat.
I knew it was a matter of time.
The night I was sterilised by a surgery that went terribly wrong, I found out he was cheating.
I told him to uproot.

Another came.
This time-this time-I wouldn't need to escape or uproot.
Wouldn't get battered or twisted.
But, when sickness came again, he uprooted.
And while I dangled, I wasn't destroyed.
I didn't collapse, although I did spill out my leaves a bit.
While I moved "way out west", I didn't become bitter.

I became bigger.
I found ways to hold enough space for the things that blemished and tangled me.

I found ways to hold enough space for the ones who wrought the winds of injuring storms.
I uprooted the need to uproot...
Well, partly.

Likely these days I'd be doing that again.
Except I have an anchor now.
A Harbour.
And one day she may uproot from me, such is the nature of the foster system.
But for now?
For now we're planted.

And through it all I've learned winds will come.
Brutal, decimating, winds.
And you'll be shaken, tossed, bent.
Parts of you-your life- collapsed and now debris across the path ahead.
You may have no choice but to stay.
To uproot.
To twist, tangle, and break.
But you have the choice to be bitter.
Or to be better.
To be less than what you were.
Or to be more.

Fifteen

A screech that rivals a Stuka dive bomber reverberated throughout my Haven in the Woods. Bilbo Baggins and Griffin looked at me.
I looked at them.
"What **WAS** that?!" we all silently asked each other.
And then the raspberries began.

This is how my daughter Harbour wakes up. Happily squealing and chattering.
The doggos, for their part, tend to joyfully wake, too.
After a few seconds of over exaggerated stretches they throw themselves onto the floor as they shimmy and scratch their way across the carpet.
Baggings, singing the song of his basset brethren as he rubs his jowls.

I'd like to think my three Musketeers take their cues from me as I often start the day with a "Wake and Shake" myself.
Show tunes get sung.
Dancing gets performed.
Coffee-quality coffee, ya'll- gets made.
But lately I've struggled more.

Folks know a lot about my dystonia.
How I had to relearn to walk and talk.
How my hands shake and my accent is undefinable.
How I beat the prognosis of being severely deformed.

And it is a story of success, absolutely.
But that's not to say I don't have symptoms.
That I don't have setbacks.

That the pain in my jaw that causes the accents folks are so intrigued by is often so intense that it changes the shape of my face.
That it fractures my teeth.
That the tremors in my hands make it frustrating to type these Mullings.
That the twisting of my muscles in my leg feel as if my shinbone may fracture, too.
Folks hear the accent.
They don't- unless they look very closely- see these other things.
And so it reminds me of the things we don't see in ourselves sometimes, too.

My friend Cara brought an incredible insight this week that has had me even more reflective than usual: The first thing we lose when Burnout grabs hold is our sense of humour.
It's the last thing to return once we recover.
Goodness, ya'll, do I believe that.

As I think upon Cara's statement, I think about the things that have historically led to some of my worst dystonia flares.
Emotional stress.
Traumatic events.
Unreasonable and unsustainable expectations.
They led to Burnout, too.

And, along with the inability to control my muscles, I also lost my sense of humour.
Oh, sure, I was snarky and deprecating, but I wasn't funny.
Glib, not clever.
And it has taken me almost as long as it took me to defy the dystonia odds, to get my humour back.

So now that I know this, and I've regained my happy hilarity, I'm not ever letting it leave me again.

Some of the factors that led to my Burnout may return.
I may have setbacks.
I may have symptoms.
And, you know, dystonia is something I cannot control.
I cannot corral the inputs of the myriad stressors that contribute to it.
But the effects of it?
That I can.

So whether it's Burnout or one of my health issues, the stressors that feed into it cause detrimental reactions.
And it's the reactions that I can control.
And, if nothing else, dadgummit, I never want to not be funny again.

Sixteen

I wouldn't say I'm afraid of the dark so much as I've got a healthy skepticism of it. I'm pretty sure this all stems back to a distinctive incident one evening in my childhood bedroom.

You see, I had heard the phrase "skeletons in the closet" and my expansive childhood imagination created a glowing, rattling, creature standing just inside the open, gaping, maw of darkness that had only hours before housed the troll jumper my Nana had made me.
Totally frozen with fear, the only movement I could muster was to hug my Teddy Ruxpin closer.
Eventually, my imagination wore out and I went to sleep.
Either that, or the apparition decided to haunt someone else.
Hard to know for certain with the questionable reliability of childhood memories, ya'll.

Regardless, I've hence been the person who cannot go to sleep unless all doors are closed in my bedroom.
Except for when I'm in a hotel or rental.
In which case, in those unfamiliar places, your girl needs the door open to act as a nightlight.
Last night as my woods were lit up by a beautiful thunderstorm and disrupted fireflies that made it look as if twinkle lights had been hung throughout the forest, I reflected on all of this.
My solar lights shone around the Haven and the battery-powered timed lights I have staged throughout the main floor also kept the house aglow.
And then the power went out.

A few weeks ago one of my doctors asked if I felt hopeless.
"No. Not hopeless. Helpless." I replied without pause.

Recounting that to another on my medical team they added, 'I don't think you give yourself enough credit for just how impactful the hard introspective work you've been doing these last years has helped. With all you're up against, helpless would've turned to hopeless very quickly. You're in dark times, but you keep shining light."

A few days ago a friend asked me how they could help.
"Honestly? Just keep praying. I feel like multiple
Atlas' holding up multiple worlds."
In other words, "Keep being a nightlight."

Being a new mom to a precious bebe who is rapidly growing with each day bringing new developments is tough.

Being a new single mom is tough.

Being a new single mom stuck in a foster situation where we can be jerked around at any moment? Tough.

Being a new single mom stuck in a foster situation running my own business? Tough.

Being a new single mom stuck in a foster situation running my own business, and navigating 3-5 important medical appointments every week? Tough.

Being a new single mom stuck in a foster situation running my own business, navigating 3-5 important medical appointments every week, with an unpredictable body and health?
So.
Damn.
Tough.

And that's nothing to say of the obstinate #BadNewsBasset or #GriffinTheTerrible, ya'll!
I cannot shut the doors on these things.
But I can keep looking for light in these unfamiliar terrains.
Thank you all for being so many lights that rival the landscape of what I saw throughout my woods last night.
Je suis reconnaissant.

Seventeen

Stars are born of chaos.
People, too, really.
I mean, considering we came from all that messy, chaotic, expansive, galactic mélange.

"That's still a thing?!"
'Yes, Rach, it's still a thing.' I sighed as I read the glucometer.
It's two years of unexplained hypoglycemia. A year since a gruelling 72-hour hospitalised fast where I was stuck on the hour, every hour.
No answers.

But you know, I was used to that.

We had no answers when, after a late-term miscarriage and before my 30th birthday, I had no other option than to be steralised.
No answers why, for five years now, it is too painful for me to eat solid foods, my stomach swelling to the size of advanced pregnancy. A cruel joke of the cosmos, that.
No answers for the scars on my liver.
No answers for the lesions on my brain.

Aside from one specialist with an exceptionally misaligned ego, all eyes are pointed to Mayo's geneticist.
"I worry you're putting your hope on them finding an answer for it all." My favourite doctor said.
'I'm prepared for any of three possible outcomes. All of which will equally emotionally bereft me and I'll need time to cocoon as I grieve. But any of which actually bring hope, too.'
Her face lit up.

I originally was referred to Mayo this time last year. My doctor, desperate, sent in 5 referrals to various specialties. Genomics was interested and I eventually got an appointment in December.

When the geneticist walked in I was surprised as he said, 'Tell me about your GI issues.'
I thought "No, I'm here for the hypoglycaemia. I already have three GI doctors!"
But as we began to talk, a picture emerged.
Maybe it wasn't a series of random, unexplained, conditions.
Maybe it was one.
Smooth muscle?
Maybe.

On April 10th they began the 2-3 month long process of whole genome sequencing.
For half my life I've been waiting for answers.
For the past several weeks researchers have been intimately familiar with the cosmic chaos of my story.
Once the lab is done, the data gets pushed to me and my doctor at the same time.
More waiting until I hear his interpretation and recommendations.

"I think we're going to find something. But I need you to know that if we don't? It's because there's still a lot we don't know about all these genes. Your DNA will then get sent to our research wing as we learn more."

It has been a very long, hard, chaotic road.
I think of the times I was medically gaslit.
And the times that a doctor cried with me, us both wishing there was more they could do.

The times I've been scared and alone in waiting rooms, recovery rooms, hospital rooms.
The times I've frantically held the hand of a nurse or doctor, the tears in my eyes conveying words my mouth could not.
And the times they've later come to my room to ask about my work and research.

There's this beautifully resonating song by Dawes, "Little Bit of Everything", that keeps playing.
And, I wait here, with this.
With Harbour.
With all the chaotic dust.

Happy Growing,
M.

References

Preface:
John Densmore.
"This book is my truth. It may not be the whole truth, but it is the way I saw it. From the drum stool."
Riders on the Storm: My Life with Jim Morrison and the Doors. Densmore, John. Delacorte Press, 1990.

Fall:
Gerry Spence. https://www.goodreads.com/quotes/13260-i-would-rather-have-a-mind-opened-by-wonder-than

Krishnamurti.
"It's no measure of health to be well adjusted to a profoundly sick society." https://kfoundation.org/it-is-no-measure-of-health-to-be-well-adjusted-to-a-profoundly-sick-society/

Battle of Wounded Knee.
"They fired rapidly but it seemed to me only a few seconds till there was not a living thing before us". https://thehistoryherald.com/articles/american-history/civil-war-american-indian-wars-pioneers-1801-1900/wounded-knee/

Black Elk.
"The End of the Dream" (1932). First printed in Black Elk, Black Elk Speaks (New York William Morrow & Company, 1932). Reprinted as Black Elk, *Black Elk Speaks: Being the Lift Story of a Holy Man of the Oglala Sioux: As Told Through John G. Neihardy* (Flaming Rainbow) (New York: Pocket Books/Bison Books, 1972), pp. 224-30.

Shawshank Redemption.
Darabont, F. (1994). *The Shawshank Redemption*. Columbia Pictures.

Winter:
Horatio Spafford.
https://www.cocdiscipleship.org/middle-ages/horatio-gates-spafford-the-story-behind-the-hymn-it-is-well-with-my-soul/

Spring:
Julius Caesar.
https://platosmirror.com/julius-caesar-it-is-easier-to-find-men-who-will-volunteer-to-die-than-to-find-those-who-are-willing-to-endure-pain-with-patience-julius-caesar/

Summer:
Paul Harvey.
https://archive.org/details/Paul_Harvey_The_Rest_Of_The_Story

General Colin Powell.
https://www.usatoday.com/story/news/politics/2021/10/18/general-colin-powells-famous-rules-and-quotes-leadership/8512414002/

Franz Kafka.
https://thecitesite.com/authors/franz-kafka/

Zach Bryan.
https://genius.com/Zach-bryan-oklahoma-city-lyrics

Stay Tuned

The next book in this collective memoir is *"My Heart Sits With Yours"*.
This post on January 7, 2023 starts it off...

My father would've been sixty-six today.
In two days, he'll have been gone for eight months.

Daddy's work ethic was immense. He taught me that leadership means you assume the responsibility for the livelihoods of those you lead. That you have to ensure they have the tools and resources to succeed. And if you need to part ways?
Well, never for one second forget that you've just taken food off their table, turned off their utilities, and repossessed their car/home.
"So Wink, if you terminate an employee, you must be absolutely certain you did everything in your power to help them succeed." He taught me this, because he saw it.

He grew up in a volatile home and, escaping a stepfather who shot him, he dropped out of high school and went to work.
He married my mother and with my sister on the way, he started bricklaying... only the stone mason he worked for couldn't seem to keep his finances in order and Daddy's paychecks bounced.
My mother's father, my GDad, invested in my father to start up West Masonry.
It ran for 47 years under Daddy's leadership- all the way until two weeks before his death when my brother-in-law took over West Hernandez Masonry.

Daddy hired people with records.

People with substance abuse.

People who were just traveling through.

And that cast of characters, The Crew, became part of our family.

Daddy was tough on them, often using language that I'd gently try to coach him on (it never took, by the way!), but he gave second, third, infinite chances.

If they gave effort, Daddy would help.

He didn't discard people for a mistake or going through a rough patch. He developed.

So when it was time for me to dedicate my PhD dissertation in Human Resource Development, I knew it would be dedicated to my father.

Because that's what he did, you know?

Develop people.

As my father was passing, The Crew members of almost half a century passed through my parent's home.

As I gave his eulogy, I got to thank them for walking alongside him all those years, as well as all the contractors who took a bet on a long-haired Cherokee just starting out in the world and trying to provide for his family and his crews.

And one by one, all those men walked to the table where we had placed my Daddy's masonry trowel, and they held the handle in their hands.

Later, my brother-in-law told us why.

"After a while, the handle forms to the mason's hands. We were all just shaking Johnny's hand one last time-thanking him for taking care of us all these years."

You want to know why Leadership is so indelibly personal to me?

Why I cannot separate my field of study, my work, from who I am?
Then let me tell you all about my Daddy and GDad, and what they taught me.
It might take some time.
Bring coffee.

-M.

#MullMentum
#NarrativeLeadership
#GenerationalMentorship

Printed in the USA
CPSIA information can be obtained
at www.ICGtesting.com
CBHW032323220824
13473CB00002B/61